T0001302

To

From

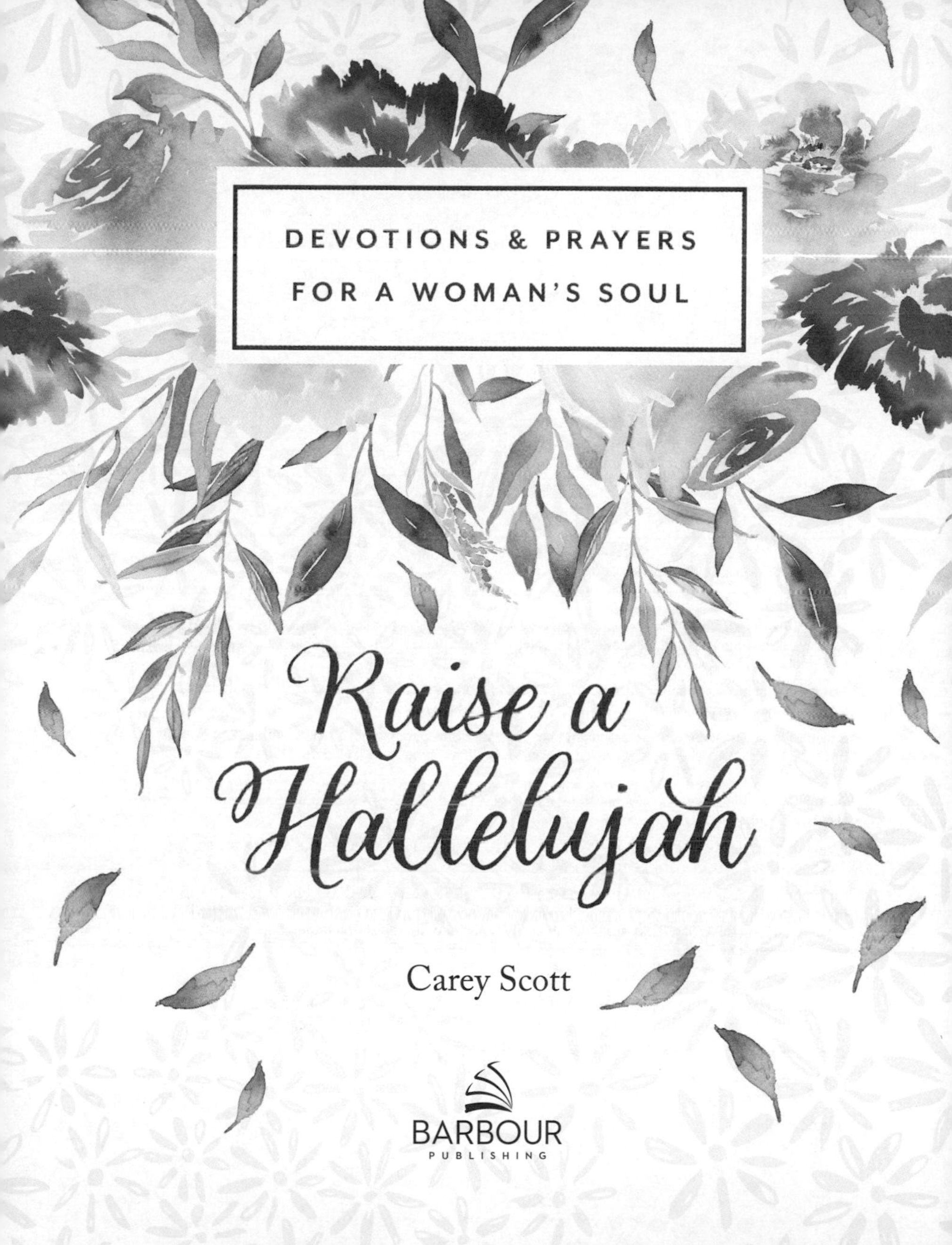

DEVOTIONS & PRAYERS FOR A WOMAN'S SOUL

Raise a Hallelujah

Carey Scott

BARBOUR PUBLISHING

ISBN 978-1-63609-260-7

Cover Design: Greg Jackson, Thinkpen Design

Published by Barbour Publishing, Inc., 1810 Barbour Drive, Uhrichsville, Ohio 44683, www.barbourbooks.com

Our mission is to inspire the world with the life-changing message of the Bible.

Printed in China.

Introduction

You always have a reason to praise God. Whether you can see it or not, He is actively and lovingly working in your life right now. His holy hand is moving in your circumstances. And the Lord is making good on every promise made to you through His Word as well as the ones whispered into your heart. Quickly raise a hallelujah in gratitude, because you are seen. You're fully known by the One who created you. And right now, God is working all things together for your benefit and His glory. Celebrate!

God Is Omnipresent

Hallelujah! Yes, praise the Lord! Praise him in his Temple and in the heavens he made with mighty power.

PSALM 150:1 TLB

Not only is God with you right now, but He is also in His temple in the heavens. He is omnipresent, meaning He is fully present everywhere at the same time. God isn't half with you and half with others. You don't get a quarter of His attention or an eighth of His time. You don't have to wait in line or take a number to know when it's your turn to talk to God. And you're never without His presence. Because of the Lord's supernatural abilities we can't begin to comprehend, He is 100 percent with His children as well as fully present in the heavens and throughout the earth. That means you are never alone, friend. So praise Him today for His omnipresence. What a blessing to us all!

God, I don't know how You do it, but I sure am glad You do! What a gift to know I always have full and complete access to Your presence. That knowledge alone settles my anxious heart. In the name of Jesus. Amen.

A Steady Stream of Praises

So we no longer offer up a steady stream of blood sacrifices, but through Jesus, we will offer up to God a steady stream of praise sacrifices—these are "the lambs" we offer from our lips that celebrate his name!

HEBREWS 13:15 TPT

What does it mean to offer up a steady stream of praises? It means you recognize God's hand in your life. And because the Word tells us that all good things come from Him, then doesn't it make sense He should receive praises for each one? So when the medical treatment works, thank God. When your child is accepted into the program or the promotion comes through, give Him the glory. When the bill is much lower than expected, your house sells for asking price, your marriage is restored, or the weather cooperates for the outdoor picnic, let God know you are grateful. Give Him your steady stream of praises, and celebrate His uncompromising goodness in your life.

God, what a great reminder that You are the giver of all good things and worthy of praise! Help me confidently recognize You each time something good happens. In the name of Jesus. Amen.

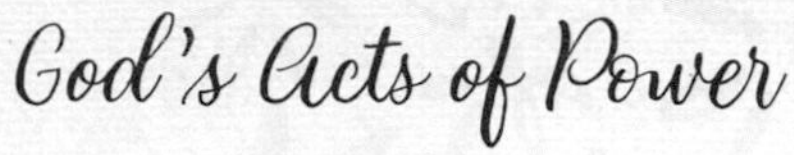

God's Acts of Power

Praise him for his acts of power, praise him
for his magnificent greatness.

PSALM 150:2 MSG

What acts of power have you seen God perform in your life? Where have you seen His hand move mightily in your circumstances? Maybe you had the courage to stand up and speak out against an injustice. Maybe you received an unexpected windfall of cash to help cover the bills. Maybe scholarship money came in to cover your child's tuition. Maybe a door opened up for a new job that's a perfect fit. In God's greatness, He orchestrates the right blessings at the right time for those who love Him. In pleasant and tough seasons alike, the Lord knows the right moment to reveal His magnificent power. Ask for the spiritual eyes to see these moments, and be quick to recognize what He has done. And remember to tell God the reasons His help made all the difference.

God, as I look back at my life, I can see clearly where You mightily showed up and changed the trajectory of my circumstances. Thank You for knowing exactly what I need when I need it. You are brilliant! In the name of Jesus. Amen.

Praise through Serving

Serve the LORD with gladness; come before
His presence with singing.

PSALM 100:2 NKJV

Did you know that serving the Lord with your time can be an act of praise? When you use your God-given skills and talents to further His kingdom, He is delighted! Every time you are His hands and feet to the world, God is pleased. Opening up your schedule to bless others never goes unnoticed. And when you prioritize helping others in their need, the Lord nods in satisfaction. But the key ingredient is gladness. Serving out of frustration or annoyance doesn't praise God. It's important your heart is in the right place and your motives are pure. Be filled by spending time in His presence through prayer. And let the Lord infuse you with joy and happiness to be doing His work here on earth. Let your service be a form of praising the God who deeply loves you.

God, ministering to the world on Your behalf is a privilege. It's my joy to bless others the way You have richly blessed me. Please see my service as praise for all You've done, and let me feel Your delight in ways that encourage me. In the name of Jesus. Amen.

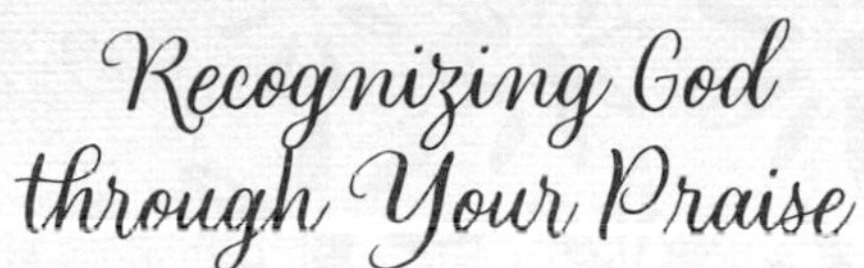

Recognizing God through Your Praise

Let them express praise and gratitude to Your amazing and awesome name—because He is holy, perfect and exalted in His power.

PSALM 99:3 VOICE

Aren't you grateful to be serving a God who is holy? One who is perfect and glorious in every way? And how awesome to be able to witness His power in your life and in the lives of those you love. Have you shared your appreciation with Him lately? It's so important to recognize God through your praise. Just as we appreciate being acknowledged when we help others, He does too. Raising a hallelujah to our Father in heaven lets Him know we understand the role He played in our situation. It's a way of honoring God for who He is and all He's done. Take a moment today to remember how the Lord has impacted your life this past week, and then praise Him.

God, forgive me for not recognizing You the way I should. As I think of all the ways You've blessed me, I'm overcome with gratitude. Hear my praise today as I remember the times I have seen You move. In the name of Jesus. Amen.

The Many Ways of Praise

Praise with a blast on the trumpet, praise by strumming soft strings; praise him with castanets and dance, praise him with banjo and flute; praise him with cymbals and a big bass drum, praise him with fiddles and mandolin.

PSALM 150:3–5 MSG

Today's verses remind us that praise comes in many different forms, so don't limit yourself! As long as your heart is in the right place, worship Him in your own style. Do you dance? Are you musical and play instruments? Maybe you're artistic, and your idea of praising the Lord is through a paintbrush and a blank canvas. Maybe you pray through singing, lifting your voice to the heavens in gratitude. Are you a writer and like to spend time stringing together beautiful sentences of God's faithfulness? Or maybe you prefer to sit in silence and think through the ways He has made a difference in your life. Regardless, find what works best for you, and raise your hallelujah!

God, I appreciate that praise can look different for everyone. You created me to be unique, and that means the way I worship You may look different from the way others worship. And that's okay. In the name of Jesus. Amen.

Facedown before God

So everyone, exalt the Lord our God facedown before his glory-throne, for he is great and holy.

PSALM 99:5 TPT

Have you ever prayed to God while flat on your face? Being prostrate before the Lord is a position of humility. It's recognizing God as Creator and you as creation. It lets Him know you surrender to His unshakable authority in your life. And as you lay facedown and recount His goodness, that act of worship will fill your heart with love for the Lord. It can be a powerful moment indeed. From recognizing restored relationships to financial blessing to newfound confidence, don't let anything keep you from giving God the glory. Whether in that moment or at the end of the day, make time to acknowledge the ways the Lord has impacted your day.

God, I recognize that You are great and holy. There is none like You. None above You or beside You. I acknowledge You as the one true God. And I'm grateful You love me enough to show up time and time again. I bow to Your name alone because You are the only One worthy of my praise. I love You! In the name of Jesus. Amen.

The Credit Is His

Know that the Lord, He is God; it is He who has made us, and not we ourselves; we are His people and the sheep of His pasture.

PSALM 100:3 NKJV

It's easy to claim success for what we do. When we score on the field, pass the exam, or land the job, so often we praise ourselves. We pat ourselves on the back for raising good kids and having a marriage that thrives. We take credit for our good health, negotiated deals, and work in the community. And while each of these situations requires our time and effort, when we take full credit, we're being selfish. God is intricately involved in our life. He created us with the right temperament and talents for the life we are to live, but He also planned to be involved throughout. Today, think about how God has worked behind the scenes to line things up, and be filled with awe.

God, help me remember that You are God, and I am not. I'm grateful for the way You created me, and I give You the credit and praise for the wonderful things I've been able to do because of how I'm made. In the name of Jesus. Amen.

Not Left Out

No one should be left out; let every man and every beast—every creature that has the breath of the Lord—praise the Eternal! Praise the Eternal!

PSALM 150:6 VOICE

While there may be times you feel unworthy to praise the Lord, the truth is that nothing precludes you from it. Don't let guilt or shame stop you from worshipping God. Shut down the voices that tell you you're not good enough. Close your ears to the lies saying your current season of sinning disqualifies you. Sometimes the best thing you can do is shout out your praises to God. Doing so has a way of changing your heart by breaking through the walls closing in on you. It turns your focus from inward to outward, reconnecting you to the Lord's goodness. And so often, that's exactly what you need to live once again in the freedom Jesus' death provided you.

God, there are times I feel unworthy of talking to You, much less praising Your name. I feel ashamed for the way I'm living my life. I feel guilty for things I've done. But from now on, I'm going to praise You even louder to break those chains of bondage. In the name of Jesus. Amen.

Lift Up and Celebrate God

Lift up the Eternal our God in your hearts, and celebrate His goodness at His holy mountain, for the Eternal our God is holy, perfect and exalted in His power.

PSALM 99:9 VOICE

It's important we take the time to lift up God and celebrate His goodness. Too often we forget to thank Him for being the solution to our problems. We don't notice His hand in our situation. We credit earthly remedies for the good things that happen to us. Or we decide things worked out because of our own choices or actions. God has an array of tools He uses to bless those who love Him. Sometimes it's people who are kind and helpful. It could be tough situations that force us to face an issue. Maybe it's treatments or medicine. Regardless, recognize God's toolbox, trusting He can use all things any way He wants. So whether you experience good through your hands or another's, your choice or another's idea, earthly answers or not, recognize that God is good.

God, I realize that no matter how the good comes about, You are the One to make it so. Thank You for being in all the details. In the name of Jesus. Amen.

He Never Changes

Jesus, the Anointed One, is always the same—
yesterday, today, and forever.

HEBREWS 13:8 TPT

We live in an ever-changing world. What was in style last season isn't today. The traditions we once held dear aren't something we cherish anymore. The world's definition of morality changes, ebbing and flowing all the time. What society considers acceptable never stays the same. And even our own relationships fluctuate throughout the years. Sometimes these changes are destabilizing because we want things to be predictable. But nothing stays constant—except God. Which is why we can anchor our faith in Him! We may not know His answer, but we know God will respond. We may not know how He will save or restore us, but we know He will. Praise Him for being reliable. Thank the Lord for His dependability in a world that never is.

God, I find my security in the truth that You are always the same. It's not that You are predictable, but Your faithfulness is. Your promises are. Your steadfastness comforts me because the world changes all the time, and I'm challenged to remain hopeful because of it. I praise You for knowing the value of being steadfast. You're simply amazing. In the name of Jesus. Amen.

Holy Holler of Hallelujah

Lift up a great shout of joy to Yahweh! Go ahead and do it—everyone, everywhere!

PSALM 100:1 TPT

Have you ever shouted your praises to God? Maybe in your car on the drive home or in the shower. Maybe in an empty field or in your basement. Or maybe you jumped up and down with a friend, screaming because something wonderful just happened. There is freedom in shouting at the top of your lungs. It's a release that's often exhilarating. Let today's devotional be a challenge to give a holy holler of hallelujah the next time God moves in your circumstances. Lift up a great shout, friend! Praise Him for healing. Praise the Lord for unexpected resources that just showed up. Praise Him for open as well as closed doors. Scream with joy at the return of a wayward child. Shout about God's goodness in offering new beginnings. Don't be shy or afraid. Take a deep breath and let it out with gusto!

God, I stand in awe of who You are and all You've done in my life. You are wonderful, and my heart is full of gratitude as I celebrate Your faithfulness in my life. In the name of Jesus. Amen.

Speak a Hearty "Thank You"

Enter with the password: "Thank you!" Make yourselves at home, talking praise. Thank him. Worship him. For God is sheer beauty, all-generous in love, loyal always and ever.

PSALM 100:4–5 MSG

What miracles have you witnessed in your life? Where has God been unwaveringly loyal? How has He been kind and generous to you? If you were to really think over your life, chances are you'd find countless ways God has revealed His faithfulness. But while you're in the thick of a challenging situation, it can be difficult to see that you are indeed held by the Lord. The heaviness of the situation keeps your eyes from noticing the work being done on your behalf. So rather than exhale in faith, you go into fix-it mode. Let this be a red flag to step back and look for God. He is always fully there with you. Begin to praise Him in faith, choosing to believe in His promises. Speak a hearty "Thank You" as you choose to trust His loyalty and love.

God, forgive me for not making the time or effort to see Your hand in my life. I know You are faithful and generous to me. I know You love me and are always for me. In the name of Jesus. Amen.

Be Vocal!

My mouth's full of great praise for God, I'm singing his hallelujahs surrounded by crowds, for he's always at hand to take the side of the needy, to rescue a life from the unjust judge.

PSALM 109:30–31 MSG

Don't stay quiet when you see God move. Don't hide His goodness from others. Sometimes a testimony of how He has moved in mighty ways is exactly what we need to hear because it builds courage to help us get to the other side of the tough season we're walking through. So be vocal about the ways God blesses you. To anyone who will listen, talk about what you saw Him do in your circumstances. Praise His name when the opportunity arises, and boast in His faithfulness to save. What better way to encourage those who need it the most!

God, You are so good to me. You are loving and mighty without fail. I want to shout Your awesomeness throughout the earth, letting others know how much You care for those who love You. Open my eyes to opportunities to tell of Your goodness. Open doors for me to brag about who You are. What a privilege to share my God-moments with those around me. In the name of Jesus. Amen.

The Power of Our Testimony

I have become as a wonder to many, but You are
my strong refuge. Let my mouth be filled with
Your praise and with Your glory all the day.

PSALM 71:7–8 NKJV

Who in your community of friends and family needs to know that God is bigger than their problem? Who needs to be encouraged that He heals marriages and restores friendships? Who is desperate to hear stories of the miraculous ways the Lord fixes financial failures and intervenes in medical treatments? Our world needs to know there is a God who loves them, One who is alive and active in their lives every day. He is our strong refuge. He is the help we need. And our testimony is how others will understand His power to be our Advocate in every situation.

God, let me be a loudspeaker to a broken world, telling of Your wonderful ways and steadfast love. Use me to reveal Your goodness to the hurting. Allow my testimony to be what inspires others to put their faith in You. And let me be free to shout Your praises to all who will listen. In the name of Jesus. Amen.

Red Sea Moment

You commanded the Red Sea to divide, forming a dry road across its bottom. Yes, as dry as any desert! Thus you rescued them from their enemies. Then the water returned and covered the road and drowned their foes; not one survived.

PSALM 106:9–11 TLB

Imagine the wonder and awe experienced by the Israelites. With the enemy behind them and the deep water in front, think about their cries to God. Consider the fear raging inside. But then He made a way by splitting open the waters and drying the ground that had been saturated by water for hundreds of years. They crossed. The enemy died. And shouts of praise ensued! Their deliverance is a powerful reminder that the Lord will always make a way for those He loves. Friend, do you need a Red Sea moment in your own life? Praise God right now and believe one is coming.

God, hear my cry today. You know the places I'm desperate for a Red Sea moment to manifest. You know where I'm looking for You to intervene on my behalf. Be big in my situation, Lord. Let me see Your mighty hand move in miraculous ways. I'm praising You now! In the name of Jesus. Amen.

Those Get-Me-Out-of-Here Moments

Oh, God, my Lord, step in; work a miracle for me—you can do it! Get me out of here—your love is so great!—I'm at the end of my rope, my life in ruins. I'm fading away to nothing, passing away, my youth gone, old before my time.

PSALM 109:21-23 MSG

How many times have you thought to yourself, *Get me out of here*? Release me from this marriage. Remove me from this job. Disconnect me from this responsibility. Detach me from this commitment. Delete this friendship. Cut off my need for validation. Get rid of my disease. Withdraw my heart from caring. Instead of looking for the closest exit—which may be God's plan in the end—ask Him to step in and work a miracle. Tell Him your frustrations, and trust He will make right what feels wrong. And then be ready to praise Him for being faithful and true, and let others into your victory so they can praise Him too.

God, help me change my perspective so I'm not always looking for a way out but instead focusing on how You will intervene. Your ways are always the best ways! In the name of Jesus. Amen.

His Ear Is Inclined toward You

Deliver me in Your righteousness, and cause me to escape;
incline Your ear to me, and save me. Be my strong refuge,
to which I may resort continually; You have given the
commandment to save me, for You are my rock and my fortress.

PSALM 71:2–3 NKJV

With all that's going on in the world at any given moment, praise God for always inclining His ear toward you. He is never too busy. He doesn't have a waiting list. Even if everyone were speaking to Him at the exact same time, the Lord is able to bring each person into a private audience. We may not understand how He does it, but we can praise Him for it, nonetheless. Whenever you cry out to God, He hears you like you're the only one. When He responds, the Lord's attention isn't splintered. And His wonderful ability to give you His undivided attention is just one more reason to glorify His name.

*God, I don't know how You do it, but I am so grateful.
Thank You for making me feel seen and known as only You
can do. I praise Your name! In the name of Jesus. Amen.*

Let Him Hear Your Voice

Help me, oh help me, GOD, my God, save me through your wonderful love; then they'll know that your hand is in this, that you, GOD, have been at work.

PSALM 109:26–27 MSG

Where do you need God's help right now? Have you asked for it? Have you spent time in prayer, telling Him about your frustrations? Does He know the heaviness of your heart? While God always knows exactly what's causing you pain and fear, let Him hear your voice. Share what's causing insecurities to flare up or what happened to make you lose courage to speak up. Open up about your crisis of confidence. Unpack the shame or guilt. And then take a breath so that when God brings help and healing, you are ready to praise Him for the unwavering faithfulness He continues to show you.

God, sometimes I don't ask for Your help because I know You already know my predicament. I assume You don't need to hear it from me. But because hearing my voice matters, I will talk to You about it all! And then I will stand in faith, waiting to worship You for being the kind of God who answers. In the name of Jesus. Amen.

Let Nothing Stop You

No matter what, I'll trust in you to help me. Nothing will stop me from praising you to magnify your glory! I couldn't begin to count the times you've been there for me. With the skill of a poet I'll never run out of things to say about how you faithfully kept me from danger.

PSALM 71:14–15 TPT

Let nothing stop you from praising God. Let nothing keep you from sharing His wonders with those around you. Don't be embarrassed to speak up. Don't let shame shut you down. It's not prideful to boast in the Lord's goodness. It's not wrong to brag on His faithfulness to save or restore. Who knows, but it might be the exact thing a friend needs to hear to give her courage to stand strong in her own crisis. Repeating it may even encourage your own heart, reminding you that God is in control. He is worthy of your praise. So. . .praise!

God, I praise You for redeeming my life! You are the reason I am still standing. I know how You rescued me. I saw the ways You came through. And I will worship Your holy name every day until I see Jesus, and then I will praise Him for all eternity! In the name of Jesus. Amen.

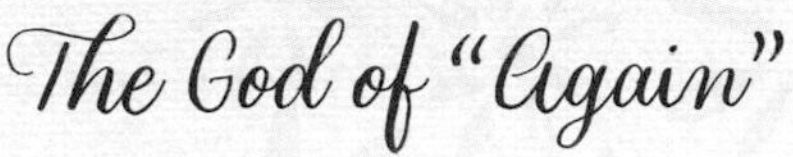

The God of "Again"

Give us even more greatness than before.
Turn and comfort us once again.

PSALM 71:21 TPT

Sometimes we don't ask God for help because we find ourselves in the same messy situation again. Rather than unpack our problems with the only One who truly understands our predicament, we end up embarrassed of our choices and think we deserve what we've got coming to us. We turn our eyes from God, certain He's ashamed of us and frustrated by our behavior. And we sink deeper in our shame, feeling hopeless that things will ever change. Raise a hallelujah that we serve a God of second chances! He doesn't tire of our humanity. That means every single time we mess up—be it a repeat or a brand-new situation—He is there to comfort us again. Friend, His heart for you is always good. And there is nothing you can do to make Him love you more or less than He does right now. What an awesome God.

God, what a relief to know You are the God of again. I praise You for being the only One who loves without fail, who is always concerned with my heart and restoration no matter how many times I mess things up. In the name of Jesus. Amen.

Who Has God Been to You?

I will shout and sing your praises for all you are to me—Savior, lover of my soul! I'll never stop telling others how perfect you are, while all those who seek my harm slink away ashamed and defeated!

PSALM 71:23–24 TPT

Who is God to you? Think about the ways He has shown up in your life. Write them down in your journal. Has God been your Redeemer? Has He saved you? Is He the One who gives you unexplainable peace? Has He been a door opener and closer? Is He a joy giver? Has God been unwavering in His faithfulness? Did He restore your heart? Has the Lord healed? Is He your confidant and strength? Your provider? Did He bless you with wisdom and discernment? Has He given you unshakable hope? Take time today to praise God for all He is and has been to you. Be specific and thorough. And tell Him how He has changed your life.

God, I'm amazed as I look at who You've been to me. There isn't one time I've needed You that You haven't shown up. I worship You because You are magnificent. Thank You for loving me every day and in every way. Your faithfulness means so much. In the name of Jesus. Amen.

Counting the Miracles of God

Hallelujah! Thank you, Lord! How good you are! Your love for us continues on forever. Who can ever list the glorious miracles of God? Who can ever praise him half enough?

PSALM 106:1–2 TLB

The psalmist says it's impossible to list the glorious miracles of God, but why don't you try? How might you delight God by intentionally seeking out miracle moments for yourself? Yesterday's devotional challenged you to look at who God is to you. Today, praise Him for how He has blessed you. Remember that scripture says all good things come from God. So if you look back through that lens, you'll be left praising God without a break for years to come. Hallelujah and amen! Glory to God in the highest! Friend, you are so loved. You are so valued. You are a top priority to your heavenly Father. He carefully knit you together in your mother's womb with great intentionality. Think of it—the Lord has been blessing the socks off you since before you took your first breath!

God, I'm blown away by all the blessings I've been able to recall. Forgive me for not seeing them before. You're an amazing Father who loves His children well. I praise You for Your goodness! In the name of Jesus. Amen.

The Hallelujah Prayer

My God, don't turn a deaf ear to my hallelujah prayer. Liars are pouring out invective on me; their lying tongues are like a pack of dogs out to get me, barking their hate, nipping my heels—and for no reason!

PSALM 109:1–3 MSG

When you feel trapped or targeted by those who dislike you, fear often takes over. Thinking of the ways their evil plans may affect you can be scary. We know the Bible confirms that we will have trouble. We'll face hardships; we aren't exempt from them. Most of us know this from our own life experience, and so we sometimes decide our new worries are justified. That's exactly why we need God to hear our hallelujah prayers. As we pour out our heart in authenticity, we tell the Lord we trust Him. And then we praise God on the front end, believing in His goodness on the back end of the situation.

God, my heart is heavy and I'm worried. I know You're trustworthy, but I need help in those moments of unbelief. Hear my praises, for I'm choosing to offer this hallelujah prayer in faith ahead of the revealing of Your goodness. In the name of Jesus. Amen.

Nothing Is Impossible When God Steps In

Our Lord is great. Nothing is impossible with His overwhelming power. He is loving, compassionate, and wise beyond all measure.

PSALM 147:5 VOICE

When we get to the end of ourselves, God takes over. He makes up the difference when we fall short. The Lord creates a bridge between impossible and possible. He adds the super to the natural. As a result, we can be full of hope for good things to happen. God gives credence to the unthinkable. He offers confidence when we face the unimaginable. The Word says nothing is impossible when His power gets into the mix. His authority to do the impractical and unfeasible will overwhelm any negativity. Praise God! With Him, we are limited by nothing. We can be full of hope even if we can't see a way forward. In His love, compassion, and wisdom, we are unstoppable.

God, You're simply amazing. You think of everything! I'm glad to know You will always make a way for the impossible to become possible. I can dream and hope with abandon, knowing Your will always will be done. I can't mess up Your plans with my human limitations. That's why I'm raising a hallelujah in celebration! In the name of Jesus. Amen.

Above and Greater

Let them all praise the name of the Eternal! For His name stands alone above all others. His glory shines greater than anything above or below.

PSALM 148:13 VOICE

Be careful whom you choose to put on a pedestal. We may worship attorneys who work to ensure that justice is served. We might lift up government officials whom we consider godlike in power. We could look up to a spouse, a mentor, or a pastor, regarding them as infallible. Maybe it's a celebrity or a big-name author or speaker. It could even be ourselves. Amen? And while we can express an honest dose of gratitude or a hearty "Job well done" comment, the only One we should shower with praise is God. He is the One whose name is above every name, the One who is greater than all others. He is good all the time, so let's praise the Lord in earnest every day!

God, forgive me for the times I've put someone above You in my mind. I never want to make that kind of mistake again, because I know You are above and greater than everyone in every way. Yours is the only name worthy of praise! How grateful I am to serve a God who has no equal. In the name of Jesus. Amen.

Floods of Trouble

God, my God, come and save me! These floods of trouble have risen higher and higher. The water is up to my neck! I'm sinking into the mud with no place to stand, and I'm about to drown in this storm.

PSALM 69:1–2 TPT

What a descriptive passage of scripture! Can you relate to how the psalmist is feeling? Have you been in floods of trouble where the waters kept rising and you felt trapped? Maybe the bills kept coming but the income didn't. Maybe you lost influence with your teenager as they continued making terrible choices. Maybe the deadlines changed, and you struggled to keep up. Maybe the medication didn't work for you as hoped. These are the moments you cry out for God to come quick and save you. This is when you call to the One who can deliver! And as you do, remember to worship Him with your words, letting Him know your faith in His power is solid.

God, I know You see me in the mud with the water rising around me. I know You have the power to save me! And I praise You for the miracle You're about to perform. In the name of Jesus. Amen.

When You're Exhausted in the Waiting

I'm weary, exhausted with weeping. My throat is dry, my voice is gone, my eyes are swollen with sorrow, and I'm waiting for you, God, to come through for me.

PSALM 69:3 TPT

Waiting on God is exhausting, and it drains us of peace and joy. Even the most seasoned Christians battle with hopelessness when God's responses seem slow. It's hard to keep standing. In the heat of the battle, there is nothing we want more than to find victory in the Lord. For some, the delay is too much to bear, and they give up. They simply don't have strength left to wait, so they give in. But it's in the moments when we're at our limit that we need God to show up over everything else. Never late, the Lord's deliverance always comes in His perfect timing. And we praise Him for it.

God, please come quick. I know You will act at the right moment, but I'm so weary. Give me strength to wait on You and keep my eyes on You. I will rejoice when I see You come, because it will mean deliverance is finally here. In the name of Jesus. Amen.

God Makes His People Strong

He has made His people strong; He is the praise of all who are godly, the praise of the children of Israel, those whom He holds close. Praise the Eternal!

PSALM 148:14 VOICE

The Lord has no expectation that we will be the ones to strengthen ourselves. He isn't counting on you to be your own cheerleader. Instead, God is the One who makes His people strong. Recognize what a huge blessing that is, because we could never muster that kind of strength without Him. Sure, we can be brave for a season. We can put on our big-girl pants for specific situations. We can grin and bear it for a bit. But when we're tossed about by life's scary storms, our only hope is being anchored in God's strength. Raise a hallelujah to the Lord for making us strong!

God, thank You for being the One to bring strength to me. I'm so grateful my strength doesn't come through my own effort, because I feel very inadequate right now. I'm weary. But I stand strong in my worship of You, acknowledging Your power and might as superior in every way. In the name of Jesus. Amen.

He Knows It All and Still Loves You

God, my life is an open book to you. You know every sin I've ever done. For nothing within me is hidden from your sight!

PSALM 69:5 TPT

If those closest to you knew every wrong thing you've done, would they still love you? Would they look at you in judgment? Would your relationship change or be different? Could you face them without feeling shame? It's important to understand God's love is different. Unlike the imperfect love of those around you, His is unconditional. The Lord knows every single sin and still adores you. He knows the shameful moments no one else does. He has the details you'd never share with others. Nothing is hidden from God. And still, His love for you is immeasurable. That fact alone is worthy of praise!

God, I'm embarrassed to think You know all the sins I've committed. How can a perfect God love such an imperfect person? So often I want to cower in shame, but I'm choosing to embrace Your love and forgiveness instead. I want to run and hide, but I know Jesus died on the cross to wash those sins away. So hear my praises rise up! In the name of Jesus. Amen.

When God Is Your Way Out

Pull me out of this mess! Don't let me sink! Rescue me from those who hate me and from all this trouble I'm in! Don't let this flood drown me. Save me from these deep waters or I'll go down to the pit of destruction.

PSALM 69:14–15 TPT

Have you ever been so deep in a mess you knew the only way out was God? Most of the time, the situation resolves itself. The heat of the moment passes, and flaring tempers simmer down. Everyone recognizes the part they played, and apologies are shared. But then there are circumstances where we feel as if we're being pulled under. It's a hopeless feeling that's hard to shake. How wonderful to have God on our team! In those desperate moments, it's His help that will rescue you. It's His strength that will pull you from the pit. It's His power that will establish you. Let your praises of thanksgiving reach the heavens!

God, please see me. Know the pain and fear I'm feeling right now. Understand the anxiety I'm experiencing. And please come quickly, because You're the only One who can help. I need You to save me. In the name of Jesus. Amen.

Your Miracle Is Coming

I am burdened and broken by this pain. When your miracle rescue comes to me, it will lift me to the highest place. Then my song will be a burst of praise to you. My glory-shouts will make your fame even more glorious to all who hear my praises!

PSALM 69:29–30 TPT

God is trustworthy. You can know without any doubt that He not only sees your circumstances but is working a plan that will benefit you and glorify Him. Every tear you cry, every anxious thought you have, every fear that rears its ugly head—the Lord is fully aware of them all. Nothing escapes His gaze when it comes to you, friend. So take heart because your miracle is coming. His answer is on its way. And when it arrives, let your shouts of praise be cause for celebration! Raise a hallelujah to the heavens acknowledging all the ways God met you in your mess and brought His sweet deliverance.

God, I know a miracle is coming that will save me from this pain. My faith is strong because I've seen You work all things for good in my life before. And when I see it again, I will give You the glory once more! In the name of Jesus. Amen.

He Wants Your Praises More

For I know, Yahweh, that my praises mean
more to you than all my gifts and sacrifices.

PSALM 69:31 TPT

When you take the time to give a shout-out to God for His goodness, it means the world to Him. Just as we crave positive attention, God desires to receive your honor and acknowledgment. He wants you to see Him working in your life. He wants you to notice the ways He cares about each detail of the circumstances you're facing. God wants you to be aware of His powerful love and protection over you, His beloved. By raising a hallelujah in response, you're telling the Lord not only that you're grateful but also that you see His fingerprints in your situation. He wants your praises more than anything else you could offer, so give them freely!

God, I praise You for all the times You've stepped in to save me. Thank You for Your perfect timing. You're always faithful to give me exactly what I need in every situation. Yes, I see Your mighty hand moving in my life, and I am in awe of how deep Your love is for me. In the name of Jesus. Amen.

His Praiseworthy Entrance

Oh, Lord God, answer my prayers! I need to see your tender kindness, your grace, your compassion, and your constant love. Just let me see your face, and turn your heart toward me. Come running quickly to your servant. In this deep distress, come and answer my prayer.

PSALM 69:16–17 TPT

A state of desperation is a horrible place to be. It's in those moments we feel as if our chest will explode. Our eyes well with uncontainable tears. We either curl up in a ball under the covers or work overtime to fix things. We struggle to catch our breath, or we shout orders in an attempt to control the situation. Regardless, hopelessness is palatable, and we desperately need God to meet us in those dark places. He is the only One who knows exactly what we need to find solid footing. Hold on for His praiseworthy entrance! It's on the way!

God, I'm struggling and full of despair. No matter how I try, I can't seem to find my way out of this mess, and I need Your help! Come quickly and save me. Set me on the path of freedom once again, and I will give You all the glory. In the name of Jesus. Amen.

We Will Suffer Trials

Through faith, God's power is standing watch, protecting you for a salvation that you will see completely at the end of things. You should greatly rejoice in what is waiting for you, even if now for a little while you have to suffer various trials.

1 PETER 1:5–6 VOICE

What trials are you facing today? Troubles in your marriage? Betrayal by a friend? Newly discovered health issues? Lack of confidence? Aging parents? The loss of someone close to you? Fear of the future? Inability to get pregnant? Longing for a significant other? A devastating divorce? Bankruptcy? There's no doubt we will all face trials of many kinds. This suffering has been foretold in God's Word, letting us know it's inevitable. But we can praise God in His infinite grace and love that all these trials will come to an end. They are not forever battles. So let Him be your source of peace and comfort through them. Thank the Lord for His willingness to walk with us.

God, thank You for setting the expectation that we will undergo trials. I praise You for being the kind of God who will never leave us to fight them alone. In the name of Jesus. Amen.

God's Word Is Forever

Human beings are frail and temporary, like grass, and the glory of man fleeting like blossoms of the field. The grass dries and withers and the flowers fall off, but the Word of the Lord endures forever!

1 PETER 1:24–25 TPT

Sometimes it's hard to grasp that we are temporary. In one hundred years, no one here right now will still be. Wow, right? And scripture tells us that without Him, we lack strength. Our frame is frail. But the Word of God is so powerful that it will last forever. The words written thousands of years ago are still valid. They're still important, and they are relevant even today! Any situation you may face is covered in the Bible. Any solution needed is found in its pages. What an amazing God to make it so! Raise a hallelujah to the One who documents parts of His story so we can know Him better. Praise to the One who meets us in His Word and shows us the way. This world may be temporary, but God's Word is forever!

God, You think of everything. Let Your name be glorified in all who read Your holy Word. In the name of Jesus. Amen.

Your Authentic Faith

But these only reveal the sterling core of your faith, which is far more valuable than gold that perishes, for even gold is refined by fire. Your authentic faith will result in even more praise, glory, and honor when Jesus the Anointed One is revealed.

1 PETER 1:7 TPT

God puts a premium on authentic faith. He loves an honest heart. You may not feel comfortable with being transparent with those around you, so let God be your safe place. If you are struggling with an addiction, tell Him. If fear has a stronghold and you can't open up to others, do so with God. Are you questioning your value as a woman? Then talk to the Lord about it. Whether you're struggling with relationships, fears and insecurities, finances, or anything in between, God is always available to listen without condemnation. What a privilege to be real with Him. How wonderful to have that kind of freedom. Raise a hallelujah to your magnificent Confidant!

God, thank You for being a safe place for me to be real and honest about what I'm thinking. And thank You for not judging me for the things I struggle with. What a gift! In the name of Jesus. Amen.

Just as He Said

O Lord, I will honor and praise your name, for you are my God; you do such wonderful things! You planned them long ago, and now you have accomplished them, just as you said! You turn mighty cities into heaps of ruins. The strongest forts are turned to rubble. Beautiful palaces in distant lands disappear and will never be rebuilt.

ISAIAH 25:1–2 TLB

The only One who has the power to stay true to His word is God. Whether they mean to or not, people will let you down. They may have every good intention to make good on their promises, but they just don't have what it takes. We are imperfect people in an imperfect world, trying to love on other imperfect people. What a recipe for disaster. Amen? Yet the Bible tells us God's way-back plans for us will be accomplished. He's simply unable to go back on His word or break a promise. And He doesn't change His mind. So save your worship for the One who will do what He says He will do, without fail.

God, I believe all will work out in the end, just like You said it would. Your plans are always for my good, and Your gaze is always on me. Your faithfulness is praiseworthy! In the name of Jesus. Amen.

Hallelujah-Raising Situations

Also at that time, people will say, "Look at what's happened! This is our God! We waited for him and he showed up and saved us! This God, the one we waited for!"

ISAIAH 25:9 MSG

What a glorious relief when God finally steps onto the scene. That moment when our cries and pleas are met with His saving power is purely magnificent. While we believed God would show up, the exact moment it happens fills us with sheer gratitude and excitement. It's a faith-building experience that leaves a mark. It allows us to exhale as we take it all in. And maybe through tears, we whisper "Thank You" to the One who loves us without fail. Let these moments be a catalyst for praising God with fervor. Let them be hallelujah-raising situations in which we recognize the awesomeness of the Lord and His timing. We waited. God showed up. And we have been saved. Praise the Lord!

God, I'm always relieved when You step into my mess. I try my best to hold on as I wait, knowing my steadfastness will pay off in the end. Thank You for staying true to Your word. I can always count on You! In the name of Jesus. Amen.

Reaping and Sowing

You love him passionately although you have not seen him, but through believing in him you are saturated with an ecstatic joy, indescribably sublime and immersed in glory. For you are reaping the harvest of your faith—the full salvation promised you—your souls' victory!

1 PETER 1:8–9 TPT

The concept of reaping and sowing is a powerful theme throughout the Word of God. And if you look, you can see it played out in your own life. When you put in the time, chances are you will see the fruit. When you keep a steady focus, it will prove to have been a productive season. When you dig in, the rewards will come to fruition. You will reap what you sow. That same concept is true when it comes to your faith. Rejoice that God will honor your pursuit of righteous living in beautiful ways that matter to you. Let His wonderful promise to reward you be what drives you to be a faithful follower in word and deed.

God, thank You for seeing my faithfulness and allowing me to reap the harvest it brings. My goal is to love You more every day, growing in our relationship and glorifying Your name throughout the earth! In the name of Jesus. Amen.

His Love Never Quits

God remembered us when we were down, His love never quits. Rescued us from the trampling boot, His love never quits. Takes care of everyone in time of need. His love never quits. Thank God, who did it all! His love never quits!

PSALM 136:23–26 MSG

There are no guarantees in life. Promises are broken. People walk away. Dreams die. Hope fails. And too often we are left flat on the floor in a puddle of tears and fears. We feel unloved, unseen, and unimportant. Sometimes it seems as if life—and everyone in it—has quit on us. The pain is almost unbearable. And then God shows up in a powerful way, and we're reminded that His love is constant. We remember the Lord's promise to be with us always. And that's the perfect time to praise Him because His love never quits. Everything earthly will expire. But God in heaven will reign forever.

God, help me remember that Your love for me won't dissipate. Nothing I do or say will cause it to dry up. I never have to worry that You will quit on me. Hallelujah and amen! In the name of Jesus. Amen.

Now You Know Better

As God's obedient children, never again shape your lives by the desires that you followed when you didn't know better. Instead, shape your lives to become like the Holy One who called you. For Scripture says: "You are to be holy, because I am holy."

1 PETER 1:14–16 TPT

This passage packs a powerful warning for us to make good choices in life. Part of walking out our faith is following God's commands as an act of surrender. This surrender is not a negative thing. It's a pursuit born out of our love for Him. Once we know how God wants us to live, we should let go of the old ways and run toward righteousness. You may think this kind of change is impossible, but when you rely on the Lord, everything is possible. His holiness is what allows you to morph into something new. Praise God for loving us enough to shape us into the kind of women He planned for us to be all along.

God, mold me into the woman I was made to be. Now that I know better, give me the courage and confidence to follow Your plans for my life. I want to glorify You in every way. In the name of Jesus. Amen.

He Calls You by Name

But now, thus says the LORD, who created you, O Jacob, and He who formed you, O Israel: "Fear not, for I have redeemed you; I have called you by your name; you are Mine."

ISAIAH 43:1 NKJV

Growing up, many of us never wanted to be called by our name. Why? Because it usually meant we were in trouble. Our parents would yell out our first, middle, and last names, sending us into a tizzy. We just knew we were about to get it. Even now, hearing our full name may catch us off guard. How amazing to think God makes His calling of our name a beautiful thing. Isn't it just like Him to turn a negative into a positive? He takes hurts and hang-ups from the past and restores them. Friend, when God calls you by name, it's because you belong in His family. You are His beloved. Take a moment to let that truth sink in deep, and then tell Him how it makes you feel.

God, what a privilege that You call me by name. I praise You for all the ways You renew and refresh things of old that often carry negative memories! In the name of Jesus. Amen.

Whole Body, Mind, and Spirit

With my whole heart, with my whole life, and with my innermost being, I bow in wonder and love before you, the holy God! Yahweh, you are my soul's celebration. How could I ever forget the miracles of kindness you've done for me?

PSALM 103:1–2 TPT

When you're pushed to the brink, you feel it throughout your whole body. You're exhausted emotionally. Your body aches from the stress. You lack the motivation to move forward that you once had in spades. When you try to muster some grit, you find you simply don't have any. In these moments, you've reached your limit and you're done. Now think about that same concept but in a positive way regarding praising God. Your body, mind, and spirit are actively praising the Lord for His goodness in your life. You're fully expressing your love and gratitude. Your life is a daily pursuit of righteousness. And you exhaust yourself in worship yet are energized by the Spirit.

God, let me pour myself out as I praise You! I want to give You everything I have in worship. You are worthy of it all! In the name of Jesus. Amen.

Divine Hedge of Protection

"When you pass through the waters, I will be with you; and through the rivers, they shall not overflow you. When you walk through the fire, you shall not be burned, nor shall the flame scorch you."

ISAIAH 43:2 NKJV

Praise the Lord for who He promises to be when you face struggles of many kinds. Let this verse comfort your weary heart and remind you of His goodness. Let it reinforce your faith in a God who is active in the details of your life. Memorize it. Write it on a note card and carry it with you. Stick it on your mirror to read every morning. And let your hallelujah rise up as you realize that your rescue and deliverance are imminent. Friend, the Lord won't ever let you down. Even when His timing is different than yours or your plan doesn't line up with His, a divine hedge of protection always surrounds you. Glory be!

God, this verse says it all. You're amazing! My heart is comforted knowing You promise to be with me through every challenge. You will protect me at every turn. Thank You! In the name of Jesus. Amen.

Upright and Firmly Planted

Now to the One who can keep you upright and plant you firmly in His presence—clean, unmarked, and joyful in the light of His glory—to the one and only God, our Savior, through Jesus the Anointed our Lord, be glory and greatness and might and authority; just as it has been since before He created time, may it continue now and into eternity. Amen.

JUDE 24–25 VOICE

God has a special way of keeping us upright and firmly planted. The world may cause us to wilt with guilt and shame. We may be uprooted by life's storms and marked by pain and heartache. And we may fall over in muddy circumstances as we carry the weight of worry on our shoulders. But God wants our roots to go deep into the soil of faith. He wants us to secure our trust in Him so we can remain standing and steady. Because when we do, we'll be clean and unmarked in His sight. Let's raise a hallelujah to the One who braces us for the winds and rains and then removes any marks left by the storms we face.

God, I praise You for how perfectly You love me. In the name of Jesus. Amen.

In Spite of. . .

You kissed my heart with forgiveness, in spite of all I've done. You've healed me inside and out from every disease. You've rescued me from hell and saved my life. You've crowned me with love and mercy. You satisfy my every desire with good things. You've supercharged my life so that I soar again like a flying eagle in the sky!

PSALM 103:3–5 TPT

Despite the way you may have lived your life in the past, you are forgiven. Regardless of the messes you've made in your relationships, God will rescue and restore. No matter the bad choices and selfish decisions, you will find healing through the Lord. Is there any better news? He is full of grace for the lost and broken. Those are the ones He came for. So rather than sit in your shame and lament all that has gone wrong, why not praise God for all He has done? Why not give glory to His name by sharing your powerful testimony of His goodness? The Lord has crowned you with love and mercy!

God, thank You for supercharging my life. I praise You for forgiving, healing, rescuing, and saving me. You are amazing! In the name of Jesus. Amen.

Chosen, Set Aside, Royalty

But you are a chosen people, set aside to be a royal order of priests, a holy nation, God's own; so that you may proclaim the wondrous acts of the One who called you out of inky darkness into shimmering light.

1 PETER 2:9 VOICE

You are chosen. Before the world was spoken into existence, you were set aside as royalty. You're God's own beloved, and He delights in who you are. Friend, let this truth soak into the marrow of your bones, because you'll need to know it when the world tries to knock you down. Cling to it with all your might. White-knuckle it when it seems all your strength is gone. Never forget that God called you to be His. Take time today to recognize these beautiful and powerful truths, and praise Him for being an awesome God.

God, in a world that is good at making me feel bad, what a gift to read today's scripture. Thank You for knowing I needed to hear these truths. Thank You for reminding me of who I am. Give me the courage and confidence to stand strong in faith! In the name of Jesus. Amen.

Bless and Praise

I will bless and praise the Lord with my whole heart! Let all his works throughout the earth, wherever his dominion stretches—let everything bless the Lord!

PSALM 103:22 TPT

Does it feel weird to say *you* bless the Lord? Maybe you don't think you have the power to do that. Maybe you think you're not worthy of it. Or maybe you've always thought God is the One who blesses, not you. Friend, what today's verse means when it uses the word *bless* is simply to endorse the Lord. In your humanness, you're unable to sanctify a perfect God. But you can tell the world how much you support Him. You can shine a light on His goodness. You can advocate and vouch for how He makes good on every promise. And at the same time, you're also praising who He is and all He has done in your life. Speak up and share His awesomeness with the world. Encourage everyone to bless and praise the Lord!

God, I bless and praise You with my whole heart! You are the King of my life, and I want everything in me to shout Your majesty throughout the world. In the name of Jesus. Amen.

When Left to Your Own Devices

So get rid of hatefulness and deception, of insincerity and jealousy and slander. Be like newborn babies, crying out for spiritual milk that will help you grow into salvation if you have tasted and found the Lord to be good.

1 PETER 2:1–3 VOICE

Left to our own devices, we are wretched creatures. Every one of us. Even when we try to live a righteous life, we fail. We fall short of our good intentions. And we give in to things like hate and deception, hypocrisy, envy, and slander. Don't be discouraged. Instead, realize that these shortcomings are the perfect example of why we need the Lord. He redeems our sinful nature and makes us clean through the blood of Jesus. And we grow and mature by spending time in God's Word. When we invest in our relationship with Him, He makes us more like Jesus. So rather than beating yourself up for not being perfect, praise God that He is. And ask Him to help you become full of faith and fervor for a life of righteousness.

God, thank You for not holding my wretchedness against me. Mold me into the woman of faith You want me to be, and let me thrive in relationship with You. In the name of Jesus. Amen.

The Power of His Love

Higher than the highest heavens—that's how high your tender mercy extends! Greater than the grandeur of heaven above is the greatness of your loyal love, towering over all who fear you and bow down before you! Farther than from a sunrise to a sunset—that's how far you've removed our guilt from us.

PSALM 103:11–12 TPT

It's hard to wrap our brains around the depth and breadth of God's love for us. Why? Because His love is like nothing we can find on earth. Think about your own ability to love. Do you love your family and friends higher than the heavens? When they let you down, betray you, say hurtful things, or walk away, are you able to continue loving them from sunrise to sunset? Can you forgive them fully no matter how many times they hurt you? The answer is no. You simply can't love perfectly—not because you're not a wonderful person but because you're limited in your human condition. Praise the Lord right now that He isn't. Because, friend, He does love you that much. His love is loyal and has transformative power to change you, heal you, and restore you. Glory be to God!

God, trying to understand how much You love me is overwhelming. But I'm so grateful You do! In the name of Jesus. Amen.

This World Isn't Your Home

Friends, this world is not your home, so don't make yourselves cozy in it. Don't indulge your ego at the expense of your soul. Live an exemplary life in your neighborhood so that your actions will refute their prejudices. Then they'll be won over to God's side and be there to join in the celebration when he arrives.

1 PETER 2:11–12 MSG

What a huge relief and blessing to realize this world is not your home! If you have received Jesus as your personal Savior, this planet is not your final destination. With the mess of things right now, who would want to live here forever? God doesn't want you to become too comfortable here. Be careful not to sink all your hope and expectation in what the world offers, because it will only leave you wanting more. Instead, show those around you what a life of faith looks like. Let them watch you walk it out, the highs and the lows. And point others to the magnificence of the Father and the saving power of Jesus. Our God is worthy of all praise and adoration!

God, thank You for time on earth to show others who You are and help them find Jesus. In His name I pray. Amen.

End Up Blessed

You don't look at us only to find our faults, just so that you can hold a grudge against us. You may discipline us for our many sins, but never as much as we really deserve. Nor do you get even with us for what we've done.

PSALM 103:9–10 TPT

Praise God for being gentle with us. He is so intentional in the way He loves and disciplines. And when He exposes an area of sin, it's not to hold a grudge or poke fun. He isn't trying to embarrass us or get even. God only reveals to heal. Friend, let's raise a hallelujah to the One who loves us with such ferocity that He promises to save us from ourselves. He simply cares too much to leave us in our mess. He doesn't want us to stew in our sins. Instead, God wants us to live in freedom, peace, and joy! And sometimes that means He uncovers areas that need to be addressed so we will end up blessed.

God, I appreciate how you reveal to heal and not to shame me. Open my eyes to see the ways You are molding me into a new woman. In the name of Jesus. Amen.

His Wounds Became Your Healing

He used his servant body to carry our sins to the Cross so we could be rid of sin, free to live the right way. His wounds became your healing. You were lost sheep with no idea who you were or where you were going. Now you're named and kept for good by the Shepherd of your souls.

1 PETER 2:24–25 MSG

Thank God for the complete work Jesus did on the cross. He let His body be broken as an act of love. He absorbed every sin—past, present, future—of every person, paying the price for each one. And that selfless act freed you up to live the right way. He made your healing possible through the suffering of His own body. His brokenness allowed your new birth. And His death allowed God to delight in His creation once again. Isn't that praiseworthy? Raise a hallelujah to the Lord for making a way for you to spend eternity with God in heaven. And praise Him that nothing can undo the powerful work He has accomplished!

God, what a beautiful blessing to have eternity with You secured forever. I praise You for making a way when there was none. Oh, how You love me! In the name of Jesus. Amen.

The Positive Kind of Flooding

Lord, you're so kind and tenderhearted and so patient with people who fail you! Your love is like a flooding river overflowing its banks with kindness.

PSALM 103:8 TPT

Usually when flooding occurs, it's destructive. It is always reported as something negative because it tends to ruin things of value. It can cut through rocks and forever change the pattern or borders of a body of water. It may even cause someone to get hurt or die. But when the psalmist says God's love is like a flooding river, it's something magnificent. The negative connotation is erased. Visualize the way that being overtaken by God's love and kindness can soften any heart. Even when we fall short, His flood of love isn't rerouted. He has a way of turning negatives into positives, righting wrongs, and bringing beauty from destruction. Praise the Lord for changing things up for the best!

God, how wonderful are the ways You love me. I can see the flood of Your goodness saturating the dry soil of my heart, and I'm grateful for the timely nourishment! Thank You for being so kind and generous to me, especially when I don't deserve it. In the name of Jesus. Amen.

The Case for Community

Talk with each other much about the Lord, quoting psalms and hymns and singing sacred songs, making music in your hearts to the Lord. Always give thanks for everything to our God and Father in the name of our Lord Jesus Christ.

EPHESIANS 5:19–20 TLB

You were never meant to be alone in life. Instead, God created you for community. That means He wants you to have a group of family and friends to do life with. In His amazing plan, being part of a community is the perfect way to encourage others in the faith because you can share testimonies. You can have meaty dialogue about God's Word. You can talk through sermons, learn scripture together, and worship with one another. It's the perfect opportunity to share the victorious moments when God showed up. Go ahead—brag on Him to those around you. Give Him thanks as a community! What a beautiful way to help build faith and friendships.

God, open my eyes to community. I am desperate to have companions to journey with me throughout this life. And I want to be with people who love You and will encourage me to grow in my faith! In the name of Jesus. Amen.

God Knows You Inside and Out

The same way a loving father feels toward his children—that's but a sample of your tender feelings toward us, your beloved children, who live in awe of you. You know all about us, inside and out. You are mindful that we're made from dust.

PSALM 103:13–14 TPT

God knows who you are. He's aware that you're a creation of His mind and heart. He understands what makes you soar and what shuts you down. He took time to think you up, choosing with great intention every detail. God decided when you'd come onto the kingdom calendar and filled you with grace and grit for this time in history. He handpicked the ingredients to include in you—the talents and treasures—and baked them right in. Yes, your Father knows everything about you and loves you without condition. God understands you inside and out and calls you His own. Let there be praise on your lips today as you thank Him for taking time to make you exactly to plan.

God, forgive me for the times I've given in to self-loathing.
If You made me on purpose, then I should embrace who
I am and give thanks. In the name of Jesus. Amen.

Don't Let Them Walk Away

My dear friends, if you know people who have wandered off from God's truth, don't write them off. Go after them. Get them back and you will have rescued precious lives from destruction and prevented an epidemic of wandering away from God.

JAMES 5:19–20 MSG

Do you know someone who has walked away from the faith? Maybe they lost a loved one and feel mad at God. Maybe they don't believe their prayers are heard, and they've given up trying. Maybe they decided God was angry with them, and they turned away in shame. What a privilege to serve a God of second chances! The reason James is telling us to go after those who have wandered off is because he knows the Lord wants them back in the fold. His arms are wide open. Be quick to respond when you see someone lacing up their hiking boots. Don't brush them off or ignore them. Praise God for equipping you with eyes to see and courage to reach out. You have what it takes to speak up and rescue precious lives from destruction.

God, use me to bring hope to those who have lost it. In the name of Jesus. Amen.

The Call to Be Unshakable

My dear brothers and sisters, stay firmly planted—be unshakable—do many good works in the name of God, and know that all your labor is not for nothing when it is for God.

1 CORINTHIANS 15:58 VOICE

This call to be unshakable feels daunting at times. Honestly, aren't we shaken all the time? We find inappropriate images on our husband's phone or uncover drugs as we clean out our kid's car. We discover we're a victim of identity theft or get fired from work. These kinds of things profoundly dampen our confidence, and we shut down, hiding out in shame from our community. Even more, we end up self-focused rather than letting our words and actions point to God. Friend, praise the Lord for His steadfastness. When these seasons hit, you can still be unshakable because your roots of faith are planted deep in Him.

God, thank You for making it possible for me to be unshakable no matter what comes my way. I know as long as I place my trust in You, I can weather any storm. Help my faith encourage others to be firmly planted in You too. In the name of Jesus. Amen.

Unbroken and Unrelenting Love through Generations

But Lord, your endless love stretches from one eternity to the other, unbroken and unrelenting toward those who fear you and those who bow facedown in awe before you. Your faithfulness to keep every gracious promise you've made passes from parents, to children, to grandchildren, and beyond. You are faithful to all those who follow your ways and keep your word.

PSALM 103:17–18 TPT

Raise a hallelujah to the God who honors the promises He has made throughout the generations of your family! He never forgets His Word and doesn't change His mind. His love stretches all the way through time and makes good on every pledge. Imagine the depth of love and faithfulness that takes! What an awesome God! You can be grateful for many things every day, but make sure one of them is His unbroken and unrelenting love toward those who love Him. Follow the Lord with all your heart, and reap the blessings that will come.

God, You are simply wonderful. I don't know how You keep track of all the promises You make, but what a blessing that You do. I praise Your faithfulness, and I commit my life to You. In the name of Jesus. Amen.

Praising in Every Moment

I will praise the Eternal in every moment through every situation. Whenever I speak, my words will always praise Him. Everything within me wants to pay tribute to Him. Whenever the poor and humble hear of His greatness, they will celebrate too! Come and lift up the Eternal with me; let's praise His name together!

PSALM 34:1–3 VOICE

The Word encourages us to praise God in every moment. That means we keep an eye out for His hand in our situation. We set an expectation that He will show up no matter what. And because we know all good things come from God, we praise Him when they happen. From receiving a marriage proposal to scoring high on your big test to finding a front-row parking space in the snow, raise a hallelujah to the Lord for His goodness. Let these blessings be part of the story you share with others too. We all need reminders that God is for us and will be faithful to provide help when needed.

God, I praise You for knowing exactly what I need and when I need it. . .and blessing me in Your generous abundance. In the name of Jesus. Amen.

God Wins

The Lord is close to all whose hearts are crushed by pain, and he is always ready to restore the repentant one. Even when bad things happen to the good and godly ones, the Lord will save them and not let them be defeated by what they face.

PSALM 34:18–19 TPT

Praise the Lord that He stands by us when we feel crushed by pain. What a blessing to know He is close to the brokenhearted. And hallelujah that our repentance always leads to God's restoration. We are lost without Him. Friend, following the Lord doesn't guarantee us an easy life. We don't get to skip hard circumstances. Difficulties won't pass us by. But God promises to save us every time so that we won't be defeated by the struggles we face. Nothing will take us down if we place our trust in God. Recognize that sometimes bad things will happen in your life and the lives of those you love. Even so, purpose in your heart to rejoice, knowing God will trump them all.

God, please come closer to me in my sadness. Help me find hope in Your goodness. I'm trusting You to restore my heart once again. In the name of Jesus. Amen.

God Will Always Respond to You

When I needed the Lord, I looked for Him; I called out to Him, and He heard me and responded. He came and rescued me from everything that made me so afraid.

PSALM 34:4 VOICE

Can you think of a situation where you cried out to the Lord and He did not respond? Scripture tells us that every time your voice calls His name, God not only hears you but answers. He may not answer in the way you want. The timing of His response may be different than what you expect. But none of that changes the truth that God is active in your life every day and in all circumstances. Even more, His holy ear is trained on your voice and always bent in your direction. Sweet one, His gaze never strays from your face. Take a minute to let that truth sink in, and praise Him for it!

God, what a gift to know You'll always answer me when I cry out to You. Give me courage to trust both Your response and Your timing even when they don't align with what I think is best. I know Your heart for me is always good. In the name of Jesus. Amen.

Every Need Satisfied

I am convinced that my God will fully satisfy every need you have, for I have seen the abundant riches of glory revealed to me through Jesus Christ! And God our Father will receive all the glory and the honor throughout the eternity of eternities! Amen!

PHILIPPIANS 4:19–20 TPT

What are your needs right at this moment? Is your marriage at divorce's doorstep and in need of a miracle to salvage it? Are your finances in a mess and you're craving relief? Do you need grace and perseverance to raise your special-needs child? Are your nerves frayed at work so you're hoping for another job? Honestly, we are all lacking in different places in life. We are all desperate for the Lord to intervene. But we can raise a hallelujah knowing God promises to fully satisfy every need according to His perfect plan. That means we can stand in faith and watch it all come together.

God, help me trust that You will come through for me again. Even more, give me the courage to trust Your plan over mine! That's the hardest part. But You are good, and I know I am loved. In the name of Jesus. Amen.

Always Seek Peace

If you love life and want to live a good, long time, take care with the things you say. Don't lie or spread gossip or talk about improper things. Walk away from the evil things of the world, and always seek peace and pursue it.

PSALM 34:12–14 VOICE

Every day you have a choice. Will you choose to follow peace, or will you follow what your flesh wants? It's often a simple decision that's hard to make. But keep in mind that choosing peace, according to scripture, will help you live a good, long life. So when you're faced with a decision, ask God to show you the road that will keep you at peace. Will you gossip, or will you stay quiet? Will you do what everyone else is doing, or will God's way prevail? If one path stirs up anxiety or fear, choose the other one. If one feels destabilizing, follow the one that promotes harmony. And thank the Lord for His peace that makes you feel secure and loved. What an awesome God!

God, help me pursue peace whenever possible. Highlight the path to take so I don't make the wrong choices. And let my life reflect my decision to follow Your plans for my life. In the name of Jesus. Amen.

The Secret of Overcoming

I know what it means to lack, and I know what it means to experience overwhelming abundance. For I'm trained in the secret of overcoming all things, whether in fullness or in hunger. And I find that the strength of Christ's explosive power infuses me to conquer every difficulty.

PHILIPPIANS 4:12–13 TPT

When you become a Christ follower, you have access to something so potent that your human condition alone cannot handle it. Instead, it's something borrowed from God. It's His superpower that courses through your veins. And it allows you to be an overcomer regardless of what you're facing. Be it financial ruin, rejection or abandonment by a loved one, a health crisis, overwhelming fear, or an unforeseen tragedy, praise God that you can receive His power infusion to strengthen your resolve to continue moving forward. He takes your natural and adds His super, and the result is an overcomer attitude that changes everything!

God, what an honor to call You my Father. Thanks for taking care of me by providing everything I need to live in victory. Your strength will help me conquer every battle that comes my way, and I'm so grateful. In the name of Jesus. Amen.

Unexplainable Peace

Don't be pulled in different directions or worried about a thing. Be saturated in prayer throughout each day, offering your faith-filled requests before God with overflowing gratitude. Tell him every detail of your life, then God's wonderful peace that transcends human understanding, will guard your heart and mind through Jesus Christ.

PHILIPPIANS 4:6–7 TPT

What an amazing God we serve who knows our propensity for worry and offers a solution. He understands how we as women are easily pulled in a million different directions with all the burdens we carry. What a loving Father to invite us into prayer, providing a safe place where we can share what's on our heart and be heard. We have space to ask for help. And in exchange for our honesty and vulnerability, we are gifted with a sense of peace that makes no sense to the world. Where others may be freaking out, we are at rest in the arms of the Lord. That wonderful peace is worthy of a hallelujah, friend. That gift from God is a reason to praise!

God, You know what my burdens are today. You see the fear and worry in my heart. Today, I'm laying them at Your feet and picking up peace. Thank You! In the name of Jesus. Amen.

It's an Act of Praise

Summing it all up, friends, I'd say you'll do best by filling your minds and meditating on things true, noble, reputable, authentic, compelling, gracious—the best, not the worst; the beautiful, not the ugly; things to praise, not things to curse.

PHILIPPIANS 4:8 MSG

When you choose to walk out today's verse, thinking on things true, noble, reputable, authentic, compelling, and gracious, you are praising God with your thoughts. Every time you choose to think the best and not the worst of someone, it's an act of praise. When you focus on the beauty rather than the imperfections, you are raising a hallelujah to the Lord. And when you choose to praise when the easier thing to do is curse, God is glorified. Friend, how you live your life matters. Every decision to follow His commands is worship. So live with great intention, making sure you are giving weight to His plan for your life.

God, help me live my faith out loud. Help me be intentional to fill my mind with and meditate on things that glorify You and not my flesh. Train my mind to stay focused on Your goodness through and through. In the name of Jesus. Amen.

Countless Characteristics of God

In fury You marched across the earth. In anger You trampled the nations. You went out to rescue Your people, to rescue Your anointed one. You shattered the head of the wicked empire; You laid him bare from thigh to neck.

HABAKKUK 3:12–13 VOICE

We are quick to praise God for His gentle spirit. We praise Him for being our wisdom and strength and for giving us what we need to get through the tough seasons of life. We recognize God as the giver of peace and joy and comfort. And we give Him the glory for the times of rescue and restoration, for they are many! But do we raise a hallelujah for the Lord's righteous anger? Do we acknowledge Him for meting out justice? Do we worship God's warrior attributes? Countless characteristics of God will meet any and every need we have personally or corporately, and we should praise Him for them all.

God, there is always something to thank You for. There is always a reason to praise Your name! I'm so grateful for the vastness of who You are because it means there are no limits to Your abilities in my life. In the name of Jesus. Amen.

He Is Coming Back Soon!

Celebrate God all day, every day. I mean, revel in him! Make it as clear as you can to all you meet that you're on their side, working with them and not against them. Help them see that the Master is about to arrive. He could show up any minute!

PHILIPPIANS 4:4–5 MSG

In a stressful moment, have you ever whispered to yourself, "Come, Lord Jesus"? As Christ followers, we should always have that eternal perspective. And while we're waiting, let's spend our days praising God for His goodness. Let's celebrate who He is and all He has done to bless us. Let's build a powerful community with other believers, encouraging one another rather than focusing on all our differences. Let's share our testimony and the ways God has changed our life. And let's always remember Jesus is coming back for us soon, and He is the hope we cling to every day!

God, sometimes I get so excited to think Jesus is coming back soon! I long for the day I get to see You face-to-face, praising and worshipping You in person! Help me spend my time wisely until then, and let my life make a difference for Your kingdom. In the name of Jesus. Amen.

Even When Life Doesn't Cooperate

Even though the fig trees are all destroyed, and there is neither blossom left nor fruit; though the olive crops all fail, and the fields lie barren; even if the flocks die in the fields and the cattle barns are empty, yet I will rejoice in the Lord; I will be happy in the God of my salvation.

HABAKKUK 3:17–18 TLB

What a beautiful reminder that we can rejoice and be happy even when life doesn't go the way we'd hoped. Why? Because our joy isn't rooted in the things of this earth. We expect ups and downs. We know in this life we will have trials and tribulations. We understand that bad things sometimes happen to good people. So rather than look to the world to fill us up, we leave that to the Lord. We put our hope in Him alone. And that act of obedience is blessed richly by God through peace in tough situations. Hallelujah and amen!

God, help me remember to set my expectations in You alone. This world can offer me nothing of value. It does nothing for my heart. And regardless of what I face, my joy comes from You. In the name of Jesus. Amen.

Worthy of Recognition

Blessed are you who enter in God's name—from God's house we bless you! God is God, he has bathed us in light. Adorn the shrine with garlands, hang colored banners above the altar! You're my God, and I thank you. O my God, I lift high your praise. Thank God—he's so good. His love never quits!

PSALM 118:26–29 MSG

Give God the glory for it all. Thank Him when you get the job. Praise Him when you pass the test. Give Him glory for lining up the details perfectly. Point to God for your epic performance on the court or in the courtroom. When the right doors open or close, exalt Him. When an unspoken need is met, take a knee in gratitude. As your heart softens and forgiveness happens, raise a hallelujah! It's so important to take a moment to recognize who God is in your life. Let's give credit where credit is due. He is so good all the time and worthy of every bit of recognition.

God, You deserve every bit of praise I can muster. I'm so grateful for Your powerful presence in my life, and I acknowledge Your goodness to me and those I love. In the name of Jesus. Amen.

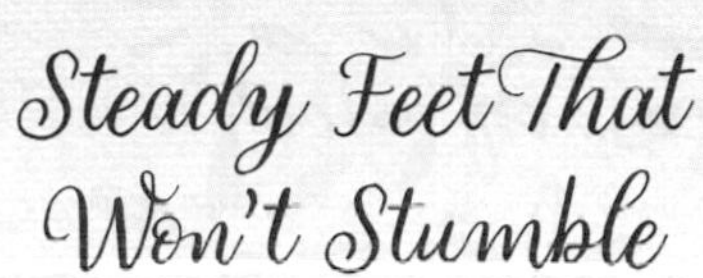

Steady Feet That Won't Stumble

The Eternal Lord is my strength! He has made my feet like the feet of a deer; He allows me to walk on high places.

HABAKKUK 3:19 VOICE

When you allow the Lord to be the source of your strength, scripture says He will make you like a deer. He will give you steady feet that don't easily stumble. Have you ever watched a deer run and jump? They are sure-footed and stable, whether on open fields or rocky cliffs. Even more, God promises to lead you over steep mountains, enabling you to walk on high places safely. Praise the Lord for helping us navigate the hard seasons of life. He will hold us up and strengthen us for the journey. God will take the lead, showing us the best path to follow so we get to the other side intact. No matter what you're facing, take heart that the Lord will help you every step of the way.

God, thank You for always making a way for me to be victorious! I know You'll always help me walk out the difficult seasons through Your strength and wisdom. In the name of Jesus. Amen.

Pray in Your Distress

In my distress I prayed to the Lord, and he answered
me and rescued me. He is for me! How can I be afraid?
What can mere man do to me? The Lord is on my side;
he will help me. Let those who hate me beware.

PSALM 118:5–7 TLB

Did you notice the cause and effect in today's scripture passage? When the psalmist was struggling, he prayed. He could have sat in his anger and stewed. He could have run to his friends for support. He could have plotted revenge or gossiped to whomever would listen. Yes, there were many different ways he could have responded to the battles he was facing. But instead the psalmist prayed to God, and he was answered and rescued. Let his story reinforce your faith that God will do what He promises to do! He is for you. He is with you. Raise your voice in praise!

God, please hear me when my heart is heavy and I'm feeling overwhelmed. Bring me a sense of calm as I trust that You hear every word I speak. Remind me of Your awesome power and might. And comfort my heart as I wait to be rescued. In the name of Jesus. Amen.

His Living Word

Let the word of Christ live in you richly, flooding you with all wisdom. Apply the Scriptures as you teach and instruct one another with the Psalms, and with festive praises, and with prophetic songs given to you spontaneously by the Spirit, so sing to God with all your hearts!

COLOSSIANS 3:16 TPT

How wonderful that we have access to God's Word around the clock, because it's alive and active today! Don't let your Bible sit and collect dust. Don't be spoon-fed through the interpretations of others. Open its pages for yourself every day, and let God speak to you. Find the answers to your questions, and dig in for wisdom. Read stories that will both encourage and challenge you. Let the truths of God's Word sink deep into your heart so they become a part of you, and watch how God reveals Himself in fresh new ways. Praise the Lord for creating His living Word as a way to connect with His children. What a kind and loving God!

God, thank You for the Bible. What a gift to have Your words bound into a book I can hold. I praise You for revealing who You are in its pages. In the name of Jesus. Amen.

This Is the Very Day

The Lord himself is the one who has done this, and it's so amazing, so marvelous to see! This is the very day of the Lord that brings gladness and joy, filling our hearts with glee.

PSALM 118:23–24 TPT

Remembering what God has done for you is an act of praise. Thinking back over His awesomeness and all the times He showed up at just the right moment delights His heart. What's more, replaying the Lord's faithfulness through the lens of gratitude shows Him how much you appreciate His hand in your life. But why not commemorate the day itself? What if every year on the same day, you praised God for saving your marriage or healing your ailment? What if that day became a cherished holiday in your heart, one you celebrated with those closest to you? This is the very day God made a mark of favor in your life. Observe it with praise!

God, make my memories of Your intervention in my life long-standing. Help me find ways to commemorate how You've blessed me. Never let my thoughts of Your goodness slip away. I want to remember Your kindness always. In the name of Jesus. Amen.

A Holy Way of Life

Since you are all set apart by God, made holy and dearly loved, clothe yourselves with a holy way of life: compassion, kindness, humility, gentleness, and patience. Put up with one another. Forgive. Pardon any offenses against one another, as the Lord has pardoned you, because you should act in kind.

COLOSSIANS 3:12–13 VOICE

We can praise the Lord with the words we choose to speak. We can sing His praises for others to hear and write them down for others to read. And we can also praise the Lord by choosing a holy way of life. Living in holiness won't be easy, but it will be worth it. When you set your mind to love God will all your heart, soul, mind, and strength, you'll find the confidence to live with this purpose. You'll be ready to forgive. You'll demonstrate grace. Compassion and kindness will be staples. You will live with a humble heart and a gentle spirit. And God will receive your praise!

God, help me live a holy life that glorifies You! Let me choose Your ways over mine every time. I want You to be praised for the awesome God You are! In the name of Jesus. Amen.

Bring It All In

Shout joyfully to the LORD, all the earth; break forth in song, rejoice, and sing praises. Sing to the LORD with the harp, with the harp and the sound of a psalm, with trumpets and the sound of a horn; shout joyfully before the LORD, the King.

PSALM 98:4–6 NKJV

When it comes to raising a hallelujah to the Lord, bring it all in! Don't be afraid to praise Him extravagantly. Praise Him in excess! Use whatever you want to glorify God and celebrate His name. Do you play an instrument? Then play it with fervor. Do you sing? Sing out at the top of your lungs! Do you dance? Then dance before the Father with pure joy. Maybe you can combine all three together and add in something else. There is no limit to your praise. There are no rules to follow. You don't have to be mild mannered or soft spoken. God is worthy of praise, and He delights when His daughters celebrate Him with abandon!

God, thank You for the freedom to express my gratitude demonstratively! There are times I want to be bold in my praise, and other times I only manage a quiet "Thank You." Either way, I want to worship Your holiness. In the name of Jesus. Amen.

Marvelous Things

Oh, sing to the LORD a new song! For He has
done marvelous things; His right hand and His
holy arm have gained Him the victory.

PSALM 98:1 NKJV

What are the marvelous things God has done for you? Did He heal you of an uncurable disease? Did He build your confidence and relieve the debilitating anxiety? Did He bring you through an unexpected divorce strong and courageous? Did He surround you with neighbors who are good people? Did He set you up in a new church where you feel loved? Did He heal your child from the effects of bullying? God loves you and is for you. Even when it seems no one else is, the Lord is on your side and ready to be your rock. Don't let any time pass between His marvelous works and your hallelujah. Don't set praise aside for a more convenient time. Raise your voice and acknowledge His goodness in the moment. Let Him know you see His hand.

God, I praise You for all the marvelous things You've done in my life. I'm grateful for the ways You intervene and bless me, often without me even asking. What a magnificent Father! In the name of Jesus. Amen.

He Is a Warrior

O Lord, fight for me! Harass the hecklers; accuse my accusers.
Fight those who fight against me. Put on your armor, Lord;
take up your shield and protect me. Rise up, mighty God!
Grab your weapons of war and block the way of the wicked
who come to fight me. Stand for me when they stand against
me! Speak over my soul: "I am your strong Savior!"

PSALM 35:1–3 TPT

You may feel surprised and even a little uncomfortable reading the psalmist's prayer asking God to be so fierce. Chances are you grew up with the image of a gentle Jesus petting a lamb. And while He certainly is loving and kind, scripture also tells us He is a warrior! Knowing this truth frees you up to pray this same kind of prayer in your situation. There are times you need God's comfort and other times you need His vengeance. You need His righteous indignation. You need His ferocity. Praise God for being everything we need right when we need it. Worship Him for making use of countless ways to love and protect us.

God, knowing You are my fierce protector is so comforting. I trust You to care for me in every way. In the name of Jesus. Amen.

There Are Times to Be Public

Then I will praise you wherever I go. And when everyone gathers for worship, I will lift up your praise with a shout in front of the largest crowd I can find!

PSALM 35:18 TPT

There are times we choose to keep the wonders of God between us and Him. Sometimes we hold them tight because they are almost too amazing to speak out. They mean so much to us that we worry sharing them will cheapen them. Yes, friend, cling to these beautiful moments. But there are other times you should go public with your praises. Why? Because a story of God's greatness may be just what someone needs to hear. When someone is desperate for a miracle, hearing that God is on the move in another's situation brings hope. You'll know when to stay quiet and when to shout from the rafters. Either way, praise Him!

God, I love knowing I don't have to share everything You've done because some things are too precious. But I also love the reminder that my miracle may be the catalyst for hope in someone else. Give me the discernment to know when to go public and who needs to hear it. In the name of Jesus. Amen.

No One like Him

Everything inside of me will shout it out: "There's no one like you, Lord!" For look at how you protect the weak and helpless from the strong and heartless who oppress them.

PSALM 35:10 TPT

When it comes to protecting you, no one can do it like God. You may not see Him in person, but He's working all things for good behind the scenes. There may be people in your community to help you through the mess whom He strategically placed in your life. You're protected by laws He allowed into existence. Through your own life experiences and education, He has developed your personal skill set with precision. So take inventory of the tools and talents available to you, and praise the Lord for each one. Just because your eyes can't look at His face or your hands can't hold His doesn't mean God isn't busy at work on your behalf. Raise a hallelujah to the One who fiercely loves and protects You!

God, I love knowing that You have everything at Your disposal and it will be used at Your command. I trust You to work all things for my good. That's just who You are. In the name of Jesus. Amen.

God Is Always There

Sing praises to the Eternal! Everyone, everywhere should know that God acts in amazing ways. You who live in this God-blessed place, this Zion, shout out and sing for joy! For God is great, and God is here—with us and around us—the Holy One of Israel.

ISAIAH 12:5–6 VOICE

What a gift to realize God is right here with us! We are never alone, even when we feel friendless. We don't have to figure things out by ourselves, even when no one seems to care. Receiving Jesus as your personal Savior means God is always with you. When you got the bad news, He was there. When their words hurt your feelings, God was there. When they walked away, you weren't alone. When the diagnosis came, His arms were around you. And the next time something goes wrong, remember God is with you. Even more, He will do amazing things on your behalf to bring good from the bad. Sing His praises even now, because great things are on the way!

God, thank You for never leaving me alone, especially in the times I need You the most. In the name of Jesus. Amen.

Choose Not to Be Afraid

See, God has come to rescue me; I will trust in Him and not be afraid, for the Eternal, indeed, the Eternal is my strength and my song. My very own God has rescued me.

ISAIAH 12:2 VOICE

Praise the Lord you don't have to be afraid of anything or anyone. Those are easy words to speak but hard words to live. Why? Because if we're honest, we'll acknowledge that so many things in this world are scary. We have no guarantees here on earth, and sometimes we feel very small and vulnerable. We're afraid of losing someone we dearly love. We worry about losing a relationship that means so much to us. We fear what will change if we lose our health or financial stability. We worry about disappointing others if we fail or fall short. We're scared of never reaching our goals or dreams. But having faith means we choose to trust God and live with the expectation of His goodness. It's a promise He makes to those who love Him. And that's why we praise Him!

God, help me keep my focus on You rather than what scares me. You're always faithful! In the name of Jesus. Amen.

Saying Thanks to God

Thank you! Everything in me says "Thank you!" Angels listen as I sing my thanks. I kneel in worship facing your holy temple and say it again: "Thank you!" Thank you for your love, thank you for your faithfulness; most holy is your name, most holy is your Word. The moment I called out, you stepped in; you made my life large with strength.

PSALM 138:1–3 MSG

Were you raised by parents who were strict about manners? Of course it depends on the family, but chances are that if you're from the South, the words *please* and *thank you* were part of your daily conversations. Using polite words was just how you honored those around you. It was how you showed respect and appreciation. So make those words part of your daily conversation with God too! Since every good thing comes from above, say a reverent "Thank You" when anything good comes to pass. When you're in the middle of a mess, tell Him "Thank You" because you know He's working things out. And when it all hits the fan, whisper a quick praise of "Thank You, God" because you know He'll be with you to the end.

God, thank You! In the name of Jesus. Amen.

He Knows Everything about You

When they hear what you have to say, God, all earth's kings will say "Thank you." They'll sing of what you've done: "How great the glory of God!" And here's why: God, high above, sees far below; no matter the distance, he knows everything about us.

PSALM 138:4–6 MSG

No one on earth knows everything about you. Your husband probably knows your daily habits and hang-ups. Your best friend may know a lot about your feelings and thoughts. Your parents may have keen insight into your gifts and talents. Teachers may see your learning potential, or a boss may notice your impeccable perception and integrity. But there isn't one person on earth who knows everything about you. Yet God does! Praise Him for caring enough to know all of you—the good and the not so good. And He loves you deeply!

God, I'm humbled You want to know me like You do. I am so grateful You care to understand what makes me tick. I praise You because I know I was fearfully and wonderfully made at Your instruction. Your attention to detail is worthy of the highest praise! In the name of Jesus. Amen.

In the Thick of Trouble

When I walk into the thick of trouble, keep me alive in the angry turmoil. With one hand strike my foes, with your other hand save me. Finish what you started in me, GOD. Your love is eternal—don't quit on me now.

PSALM 138:7–8 MSG

Have you ever found yourself in the thick of trouble, struggling to know what to do next? Can you remember when your fears and insecurities kicked in as you were scrambling to figure things out? It's in these moments that prayer should be your next move. Stop right where you are, collect yourself, and pray to the One who knows how the situation will end. God sees the entire sequence of events from start to finish, so have faith that He will deal with those against you while at the same time bringing you into a safe space. He won't walk away. He won't quit on you. Let's raise our hands and praise the God who will take care of it all.

God, I cannot imagine trying to navigate this messy life without You. I appreciate that You will be with me from start to finish! In the name of Jesus. Amen.

Sunrise to Sunset Praisin'

Hallelujah! Praise the Lord! Go ahead, praise the Lord, all you loving servants of God! Keep it up! Praise him some more! For the glorious name of the Lord is blessed forever and ever. From sunrise-brilliance to sunset-beauty, lift up his praise from dawn to dusk!

PSALM 113:1–3 TPT

Don't become so legalistic in the times you set aside to spend with God that you only praise Him then. Many of us schedule time each morning to read His Word and pray so we start the day off right. Some may do this on their lunch break as a way to refocus their heart. And others still may block off bedtime to end their day with the Lord. And while all these methods are well intentioned, sometimes we take these times too literally and ignore God the rest of the day. Why not invite Him into your entire day, from sunrise to sunset? Go ahead, take the opportunity to raise a hallelujah whenever you want!

God, please help me be less rigid and more spontaneous in how and when I express my gratitude to You! I don't need to wait to praise You. Remind me I can do it anytime I want! In the name of Jesus. Amen.

Let God Be Your Strength

The Lord is my strength, my song, and my salvation. He is my God, and I will praise him. He is my father's God—I will exalt him.

EXODUS 15:2 TLB

In those deep, dark places, remember you have a Father who sees the pain you're carrying. He knows why your heart is breaking into a million pieces. God sees the bricks of loneliness building a wall around your heart. He understands the complexities of your emotions even better than you do. Every anguished tear that spills from your eye, He catches. Every guttural sob that tears from your throat, He hears. When your stomach churns with anxiety, the Lord is fully aware of why. Friend, God is your strength, your song, and your salvation. Let praises rise up as you grasp the beauty of that truth. Let it bring comfort to your weary soul. Let it strengthen your resolve to face whatever lies ahead with grace. And be quick to recognize how God works all things for good!

God, I need You in those dark places when I feel hopeless. I need Your strength to stand strong through the storms. Thank You for caring the way You do. There is none like You! In the name of Jesus. Amen.

God's Extravagant Kindness

God's grace provides for the barren ones a joyful home with children so that even childless couples find a family. He makes them happy parents surrounded by their pride and joy. That's the God we praise, so give it all to him!

PSALM 113:9 TPT

Today's verse is a beautiful example of God's extravagant kindness and compassion toward those who love Him. It's because He cares so completely that He knows the deepest longings of our hearts and works to bring them to pass. He sees us in our scarcity and blesses us with abundance. He hears our cries and collects our tears because they matter greatly to Him. God fills us with unshakable joy and unmatched peace when it makes no sense to the world. And the Lord is generous with His time, always available to listen to what burdens our heart. Find time today to sit and recount His sweetness in your life, and let it bring a smile to your face. Then spend time in prayer, thanking Him for His help and praising Him for His magnificence.

God, thank You for seeing what's important to me and showing me kindness at every turn. In the name of Jesus. Amen.

Getting Us Ready for Life

Close the book on Evil, God, but publish your mandate for us. You get us ready for life: you probe for our soft spots, you knock off our rough edges. And I'm feeling so fit, so safe: made right, kept right. God in solemn honor does things right, but his nerves are sandpapered raw.

PSALM 7:9–11 MSG

Ever wonder why God allows hard things to happen to good people? Why doesn't He save us before tragedy hits? Why not rescue us from heartache? What could possibly be beneficial about living through grief or trauma? Consider that God in His awesomeness uses these kinds of situations to mold us and shape us so we're able to navigate this messy life. He uses difficult circumstances to smooth the rough edges in our personalities. They become tools for our tool belt, ways we can relate to the struggles others are facing. And in the end, we'll find plenty of reasons to praise the Lord for making us fit to handle the battles ahead.

God, I realize now that You allow the hard things to help mold me for life. Thank You for caring enough to prepare me! In the name of Jesus. Amen.

Recognizing God

I recognize who You are, and I praise You, God of my ancestors, for You have given me wisdom and strength. And now You have graciously revealed to me what we asked of You, for You have revealed to us the king's dream and its meaning.

DANIEL 2:23 VOICE

Have you ever been surprised when God followed through on His word? We can be caught off guard when God shows up and does what He says He will do. It's not that we don't think He can or will, but it's more that we aren't sure what His answers will look like. Rarely are God's solutions the ones we would choose. And while they are always the best all the way around, they may not make sense in the here and now. By recognizing His sovereignty in your circumstances, you are praising the Lord. Acknowledging His goodness in your life, even if you had prayed for a different outcome, is an act of worship. You raise a hallelujah every time you realize it's His hand that just moved and you call Him out in appreciation.

God, I see You in my situation, and I praise You for helping me! In the name of Jesus. Amen.

The Joy of Keeping the Ways of God

You're only truly happy when you walk in total integrity, walking in the light of God's Word. What joy overwhelms everyone who keeps the ways of God, those who seek him as their heart's passion!

PSALM 119:1–2 TPT

If you want overwhelming joy (and who doesn't?), then focus your life on keeping the ways of God. Let your relationship with Him be the passion of your heart. Want it more than anything else. Pursue it every day. And that deliberate decision will open up a storehouse of blessings over your life. Let your integrity be a light to others, shining on the things of God. Look for ways to be His hands and feet to a lost and broken world. Share your story to encourage others to hold on to the Lord for hope. This kind of living not only will bless you but also will point others to God and encourage them to trust in His faithfulness.

God, I know that true happiness begins and ends with You. I know that living in a right relationship with You brings overwhelming joy. Please give me the endurance to stay focused on Your will and ways every day. In the name of Jesus. Amen.

He Will Never Give Up on You

I will give my thanks to you from a heart of love and truth. And every time I learn more of your righteous judgments, I will be faithful to all that your Word reveals—so don't ever give up on me!

PSALM 119:7–8 TPT

Let's raise a hallelujah to the truth that God will never give up on you. No matter what you do, He will stand by you. In your worst seasons of sinning or your best seasons of shining, God will be a constant presence. Friend, what wonderful news to meditate on today! Because when we think about it, we may be hard pressed to find anyone else who loves us so unconditionally. Even the most amazing parents, extraordinary husband, and fantastic friends can let you down or fail to be there for you in the ways you need. But there is nothing you can do to make God throw His holy hands in the air and walk away. Let that truth drive you toward a deeper relationship with your heavenly Father.

God, what a gift to know I cannot drive You away.
I cannot push You away. And Your love for me
is eternal. In the name of Jesus. Amen.

Chasing After God

I find more joy in following what you tell me to do than in chasing after all the wealth of the world. I set my heart on your precepts and pay close attention to all your ways. My delight is found in all your laws, and I won't forget to walk in your words.

PSALM 119:14–16 TPT

The truth is that we will have more joy and a greater sense of satisfaction when we choose to follow God. We'll have a sense of fulfillment. In the moment, the world's options may seem like no-brainers. They're flashy and fun and offer immediate excitement and payoff. But standing strong in your faith, striving to live a righteous life that glorifies the Lord, will reap you rewards unimaginable. Your decision to set your heart on following God and His plans for your life is an act of praise. Your pursuit delights His heart! And scripture says you will find joy by chasing after the Lord and not the world.

God, keep my mind focused on following You and not the world. Nothing this world has to offer comes close to Your goodness! In the name of Jesus. Amen.

Let Nothing Deter

For even if the princes and my leaders choose to criticize me, I will continue to serve you and walk in your plans for my life. Your commandments are my counselors; your Word is my light and delight!

PSALM 119:23–24 TPT

What a relief to know we don't have to rely on human approval to secure our confidence. The truth is we will never be fully accepted by mankind when we focus on following God's commands, because there will always be people who think we're off our rocker. They won't understand why we love the Lord the way we do. Our drive to glorify the Lord with our words and actions will drive them nuts. And their critical spirits will try to threaten our sense of peace. Be strong in your resolve, staying on course to serve God and walk out His plans for your life anyway. Praise Him that His Word has the power to light the way. Delight in it as you embrace the wisdom and strength in its pages. And determine to let nothing and no one deter you from developing a beautiful relationship with the One who created you on purpose and for a purpose.

God, nothing will keep me from serving You! In the name of Jesus. Amen.

When We Need a Reset

My very being clings to the dust; preserve my life, in keeping with Your word. I have admitted my ways are wrong, and You responded; now help me learn what You require. Compel me to grasp the way of Your statutes so I will fix my mind on Your wonderful works.

PSALM 119:25–27 VOICE

Raise a hallelujah that when we need a reset, God is right there. The world tells us to pull ourselves up by our bootstraps, dust off our backside, and get in the game again. We get advice to keep going if at first we don't succeed. We're told the answers are inside us, so we need to dig deep and find them. The problem, though, is that every one of those options leaves out God. But you serve a loving Father who hears your cries for help. He sees your tears of repentance. And when you seek His ways, the Lord will open your eyes to them. Even more, He will give you the desire to follow.

God, thank You that living Your way isn't all my responsibility. I need You. Honestly, I know I'm incapable of following the right path if You don't show me the way and give me the strength to walk it. In the name of Jesus. Amen.

When the Decision Is Made

I have decided to take the path of faith; I have focused my eyes on Your regulations. I cling to Your decrees; O Eternal One, do not let me face disgrace! I will chase after Your commandments because You will expand my understanding.

PSALM 119:30–32 VOICE

What an awesome God that when you choose to become a believer, He gives you everything you need to walk out your faith. While pursuing a life of faith is the right choice, He understands it's also the hard choice. Why? Because so much of the world works against it. The world often preaches instant gratification, encouraging you to focus on yourself above all else. But the world's rules and God's commands don't align. And society's ideas of loving and serving others are often vastly different from His. But praise the Lord that you can lean on Him for help and hope. You're not left alone to walk this journey of faith by yourself!

God, I've made the decision to follow You! Be with me every moment of every day, ready to help me stay true to the amazing path of faith that ultimately leads to eternity with You. In the name of Jesus. Amen.

Turning Your Head and Heart

Guide me to walk in the way You commanded because I take joy in it. Turn my head and my heart to Your decrees and not to sinful gain. Keep my eyes from gazing upon worthless things, and give me true life according to Your plans.

PSALM 119:35–37 VOICE

When we don't know the right choice, thank the Lord, we can ask Him. If we're confused about the path He wants us to be following, what a relief to know we can ask for His guidance. In those times we struggle to do what we know is best, our amazing God invites us to ask for His help without any judgment or condemnation. He understands the tension you feel between worthless things and pursuits that are worthy of your attention. And He will turn your head and heart away from worldly pastimes and focus you in His direction instead.

God, I love that You understand the struggles I face as I try to live according to Your ways and reject what the world offers. The path is not always easy or clear. I praise You for being a constant source of grace when I mess up and wisdom to point me in the right direction. You bless me! In the name of Jesus. Amen.

Promises Made, Promises Kept

May Your unfailing love find me, O Eternal One.
Keep Your promise, and save me; when that happens,
I will have a good response for anyone who taunts
me because I have faith in Your word.

PSALM 119:41–42 VOICE

Praise be to God, He is the ultimate promise keeper. He has never broken—nor will He ever break—a promise. All throughout His Word, you see times when the Lord made a vow. . .and kept it. From Noah to Abraham to Joseph to the disciples, promises made were promises kept. Maybe God included these powerful stories to bolster our confidence in Him during our own challenging circumstances. Maybe they lay the groundwork for His unwavering faithfulness to the brokenhearted. Regardless of the why, let's raise a hallelujah that God will always make good on His word. If His promise is to save, restore, guide, forgive, strengthen, or give peace, it will happen. We may not know the when or how, but we can rest in the who.

God, in a world full of empty promises and broken vows, I'm so grateful You can be fully trusted in all things. Thank You for doing what You say You will do. In the name of Jesus. Amen.

It's Not Your Job to Judge

I watch for your ancient landmark words, and know I'm on the right track. But when I see the wicked ignore your directions, I'm beside myself with anger.

PSALM 119:52–53 MSG

How wonderful that God is a God of justice! That means we don't have to be the self-appointed hall monitor but instead can love others as He has asked. We may get our feathers ruffled, but we can rest knowing the Lord will take care of things. Rather than staying on guard, ready to tell others all they're doing wrong, we are freed up to be His hands and feet, blessing others in the world. It's not our job to criticize or sit in judgment of others' actions or lack thereof. It's not our job to defend God or His commands. We're instructed to focus on our own journey so our life can point others to God in heaven. How much better to praise Him than to pick at those around us!

God, help me remember that I don't have to defend You. I don't have to monitor the actions of others. You are fully capable of administering justice as You see fit. In the name of Jesus. Amen.

Focus Your Attention on What God Is Saying

The godless spread lies about me, but I focus my attention on what you are saying; they're bland as a bucket of lard, while I dance to the tune of your revelation.

PSALM 119:69–70 MSG

When you're the topic of lies and gossip, turn your attention away from the pain and onto God. Train your ears on what He has to say about you, not the rumors floating around. How wonderful to have a Father who is ready to listen to your heart and make healing a priority. He will bring you into a private audience as you unpack your feelings. That's the kind of awesome God we serve. In addition, look into the Word of God for encouragement. Let it inspire you. Let it set things straight in your heart and mind. Be ready for a fresh revelation to untangle the hurtful messages knotting you up. Listen to what the Lord is saying to you through its pages. And never forget to raise a hallelujah because you are deeply loved.

God, I'm tired of hearing the rumors about me. I'm tired of negativity coming my way on the regular. Train my ears to hear Your voice instead. In the name of Jesus. Amen.

God's Wisdom and Discernment

I've even become smarter than my teachers since I've pondered and absorbed your counsel. I've become wiser than the wise old sages simply by doing what you tell me.

PSALM 119:99–100 MSG

What a blessing that God doesn't mince words! He doesn't hide His will from you. Actually, God is very clear in His Word regarding His hopes and desires. It's where He shares unmatched counsel. It houses His discernment. You'll be both encouraged and challenged by the riches in the Bible. And in those circumstances where you're not sure what to do, God promises to impart wisdom to those who seek it. You may have loads of street smarts. Others may consider you wise beyond your years. You may even have a track record of using sound judgment. But every one of us needs God's wisdom to navigate this life well. We may be on track, but the Lord's discernment is what will keep us there.

God, I confess the times I've thought myself smart enough to figure things out without You. But now I understand how desperately I need Your wisdom and discernment. And I praise You for always blessing me with exactly what I need in each situation I face. In the name of Jesus. Amen.

God's Breath

I'm bruised and broken, overwhelmed by it all;
breathe life into me again by your living word.

PSALM 119:107 TPT

Can you remember a time you felt just like the psalmist in today's verse? Maybe you were going through a long and messy divorce. Maybe your child was in and out of hospitals with health issues. Maybe your best friend betrayed your confidence and shared information very personal to you. Maybe your family imploded from financial stresses and strains. Or maybe you lost someone suddenly, and their death was difficult to navigate. It's in times like these we're so thankful for God's life-giving breath that revives and restores. Honestly, there are times our only hope for renewal is the Lord. We may try to fix things ourselves, but nothing can compare to His help when we're bruised and broken. No one else can override our stressed-out feelings. Praise Him for His promise to breathe new life into you and your situation.

God, I'm so grateful You are always for me. I'm in awe of the ways You restore my heart and renew my resolve to get back up again. Thank You for breathing life into me every time I need it. In the name of Jesus. Amen.

Determined to Obey

Everything you speak to me is like joyous treasure, filling my life with gladness. I have determined in my heart to obey whatever you say, fully and forever!

PSALM 119:111–112 TPT

Deciding to follow everything God asks of you is hard. Can we just be honest and admit it? Full obedience may be a great idea on the front end, but actually walking it out is difficult at best. Why? Because it goes against what our flesh wants. When God asks you to forgive some who betrayed you, do you want to? When He tells you to love someone you consider unlovable, can you easily swap your emotions to make it happen? Probably not. So, friend, declaring this new way of living is a big deal. But praise the Lord—He will bless your quest to walk out your faith with such intentionality. When asked, He will give you the tools you need to succeed. And when you decide to obey God no matter what, His matchless peace will spill over you. You will feel His delight in your spirit. Your obedience will be worth it!

God, I have determined in my heart to obey whatever You say. In the name of Jesus. Amen.

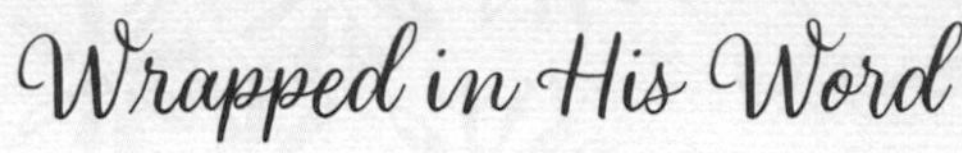

Wrapped in His Word

You're my place of quiet retreat, and your
wraparound presence becomes my shield
as I wrap myself in your Word!

PSALM 119:114 TPT

Have you ever considered the Word of God to be a layer of protection? If you will, take a moment to visualize it as a thick blanket draped over your head and shoulders. It's not a wimpy blanket but a thick one, hearty and weighty. Impenetrable. Imagine it big enough to cover you from head to toe. When you dig into the Word every day, His presence will wrap around your life. You'll be covered on all sides, shielded and protected. Sure, you'll still go through hard moments and seasons. You'll battle and struggle like everyone else. But God will be there to pull you through the mess to a place of victory. Praise God for providing a way to feel safe and secure for those who love Him!

God, I love the visual of being wrapped up in Your Word. Let that be the catalyst for me to dig into it daily and hide it in my heart. I know You will meet me in its pages every time. In the name of Jesus. Amen.

You Need God's Help

Lord, strengthen my inner being by the promises of your Word so that I may live faithful and unashamed for you. Lift me up and I will be safe. Empower me to live every moment in the light of your ways.

PSALM 119:116–117 TPT

Did you notice what the psalmist requested of God in the verses above? He asked for a strengthening of his inner being. He asked to be lifted up. And he asked the Lord to empower him to follow His ways. Reading this, we get the sense that the writer knew that in his own strength, he was helpless to live out his faith well. The truth is, we need God to help us love God. We need Him to guide our choices so we make decisions that glorify His name. Without faith, it is impossible for us to please the Lord, and the key to living a faith-filled life is reliance on the Lord's help. Let's raise a hallelujah to God, believing He will give us the ability to follow His lead and embrace His plans for our life.

God, I will give You the glory for helping me follow Your ways! In the name of Jesus. Amen.

Craving His Kindness

Turn my way, look kindly on me, as you always do to those who personally love you. Steady my steps with your Word of promise so nothing malign gets the better of me.

PSALM 119:132–133 MSG

We all need more Jesus in our life, amen? Life in this world is filled with twists and turns, ups and downs, and we need the Lord to steady us as we journey through it. Like the psalmist, we're often desperate for God to look kindly on us. We crave the way He makes us feel significant. We need the sense of calm His presence offers. And only the Lord can fill our spirit with reminders that we're fully known and completely loved. With some days feeling like an uphill battle, few things settle us more than spending time with God. He will steady our steps, encourage our weary heart, and set us back on track. Let's raise a boisterous hallelujah to our amazing Father in heaven! We can't get through this life without Him!

God, You're my refuge and safe place. You're the One who will shower me with kindness, leaving a permanent mark on my heart. I'm full of gratitude and praise! In the name of Jesus. Amen.

God Is Right!

You are right and you do right, God; your decisions are right on target. You rightly instruct us in how to live ever faithful to you.

PSALM 119:137–138 MSG

What a blessing for us to serve a God who not only *is* right but also consistently *does* what is right. In His perfection, He's incapable of choosing the wrong way. He never makes a careless mistake. He never needs a do-over. God isn't accident prone or forgetful. And nothing takes Him by surprise. Even more, scripture says He has no equal. There is none beside Him and none before Him. God is above all without question. He is worthy of our praise and devotion. So, friend, let yourself sink into His promises. Don't hold back your love and affection. Let God be your source for everything, whether you need wisdom, joy, hope, peace, strength, or patience. Ask Him to show you the right ways that lead to His love. And be quick to praise Him for being a God of accuracy and precision. What a gift to us!

God, I love that You are perfect because it means I don't have to be. My job is to follow You with confidence and faithfulness. With Your help, I can do that! In the name of Jesus. Amen.

God Truly Sees You

And should I wander off like a lost sheep—
seek me! I'll recognize the sound of your voice.

PSALM 119:176 MSG

This request is so powerful, isn't it? The psalmist is asking the Lord never to give up on him. He is asking to be considered valuable enough that his absence would be noticed. And he is asking God to pull him back into the fold if he goes astray. Friend, this isn't a tall order for the Lord. This isn't a request that pushes too far past His limits. Nope. Instead, this is what we can expect from God! You may have been written off by your friends. Your husband may have walked out on your marriage. Your kids may be too busy with their lives to give you the time of day. But God sees you! So praise Him for loving you the way He does. Give God the glory for truly seeing you. Be full of gratitude that He is always ready to restore you when needed. Yes, you matter that much to Him.

God, it does my heart so much good to know I am truly seen by You! I appreciate that You notice my comings and goings. In the name of Jesus. Amen.

Unexplainable

We cannot wrap our minds around God's wisdom and knowledge! Its depths can never be measured! We cannot understand His judgments or explain the mysterious ways that He works! For, who can fathom the mind of the Lord? Or who can claim to be His advisor?

ROMANS 11:33-34 VOICE

Praise be to God that we are unable to fully understand how He works. What a relief to know He can't be figured out by mere mortals! Wouldn't it be sad if we could comprehend everything there is to know about God? Think about it. There is something powerful in knowing God is, and always will be, uncompromised. We will never be able to understand His mind or the depths of His thoughts. He is completely unpredictable yet fully trustworthy. And no matter how hard we try to unveil the mysteries behind Him, we will never be able to. God will not be dissected or exposed. Instead, let's raise a hallelujah to the One who holds the whole world in His hands. Let's worship the One who has a perfect track record of goodness in our life. And let's celebrate His sovereignty over all living creatures, giving thanks for His magnificence.

God, I'm so thankful You are who You are! In the name of Jesus. Amen.

The God of Everything

Everything comes from him; everything happens through him; everything ends up in him. Always glory! Always praise! Yes. Yes. Yes.

ROMANS 11:36 MSG

Praise Him for being the God of everything! That means there is nothing He can't do. He can restore a marriage on the brink of divorce. He can heal a child after a life-threatening accident. He can positively affect your finances, bringing support when you need it most. God can provide a new community to fill the empty spaces. He can grow your confidence and give you courage. He can make adoption possible or bring a baby to full term. He can affect government in positive ways to further His will. The Lord can open doors to help you realize your career hopes and dreams. He can connect you with the right attorneys, doctors, and service providers. When you pray to God, asking for His help, you're unleashing His goodness in your life. Be confident as you go before Him, and praise Him as you wait for His mighty hand to move in your circumstances.

God, thank You for being the God of everything. Nothing is impossible through You. In the name of Jesus. Amen.

His Works

The works of the Eternal are many and wondrous! They are examined by all who delight in them. His work is marked with beauty and majesty; His justice has no end. His wonders are reminders that the Eternal is gracious and compassionate to all.

PSALM 111:2–4 VOICE

How wonderful to know that our God's works are marked with not only beauty and majesty but also justice. His works are countless and astounding. They point to His kindness and generosity and reveal His compassion to those who love Him. When you look back on your life and the ways God has intersected it, can you see this too? Let's be women with the spiritual eyes and ears to see the Lord at work. Let's be boisterous as we marvel at all the ways His hand has been moving in our situation. Rather than take credit or give it to others, let's instead be quick to point to God in heaven for acting on our behalf. And let's never forget to praise the Lord for who is He and how He blesses us.

God, You are extraordinary in every way, and I am deeply moved by Your goodness. In the name of Jesus. Amen.

God Will Satisfy

He satisfies all who love and trust him,
and he keeps every promise he makes.

PSALM 111:5 TPT

What an epic promise from the Lord! Grab onto this promise and hold tight, friend, because it will revolutionize your life! When you choose to follow God, showing love toward Him through your words and actions, you'll find yourself in a place of contentment. When you choose to trust Him to move in your circumstances, you'll be satisfied rather than stressed out. Because of your faith, God will deposit His peace and calm in your heart. No, your situation won't necessarily improve or be resolved immediately, but you will have confidence in God coursing through your veins. You will be filled with the ability to trust and believe. And this supernatural transaction comes from His promise to meet your needs. Let's raise a hallelujah to the One who keeps every promise He makes.

God, I know the only One who can fully satisfy me is You. Help me disconnect my heart from the world so I look only to You for contentment and nowhere else. I appreciate the way You love and care for me! In the name of Jesus. Amen.

Flawless, Faithful, and Fair

All God accomplishes is flawless, faithful, and fair,
and his every word proves trustworthy and true.

PSALM 111:7 TPT

Sometimes you may be quick to question God's answer to your situation. Maybe it wasn't the solution you had hoped and prayed for. Maybe it appears His response helped others, validating rather than denouncing what happened to you. Maybe you were expecting a bigger boom than what came. Or maybe it seems as if you were ignored by the Lord altogether. But if we believe His Word to be God-inspired and complete, then we can praise Him for things we can't see or don't understand. We can trust His faithfulness. We can believe He is always for us. And we can bring glory to God for His flawless and fair work in our life and the lives of those we care about.

God, I confess the times I have thought You forgot me or cared about someone else more. I've been critical of Your responses to my prayers, and I'm sorry. Today, I fully believe You are flawless, faithful, and fair. I believe You're trustworthy and true. And my heart is filled with thankfulness to be a child of God. In the name of Jesus. Amen.

Full Ransom Paid

His forever-love paid a full ransom for his people
so that now we're free to come before Yahweh
to worship his holy and awesome name!

PSALM 111:9 TPT

Let us raise a huge hallelujah to God for sending His one and only Son to pay our full ransom for sin. He knew we couldn't make things right, but Jesus could. And without this selfless act of love, we would be lost and bound to an eternity in hell. We'd be forever separated from the One who could redeem us. His favor would be lifted, and we'd be left to our own devices. How awful to even imagine losing the community we get to experience with God right now. Losing our freedom to approach the Lord through worship and praise would be devastating. The thought of being unable to cry out in our brokenness with an expectation of His help is terrifying. Today, tell God how much you appreciate the gift of Jesus. Let Him know that you love Him and that your relationship with Him is important. Spend time worshipping His holy and awesome name!

God, my heart is full of gratitude for Your Son's death and the freedom it affords me. I'm humbled and thankful for the gift. In the name of Jesus. Amen.

Raising the Roof

Come, let's shout praises to God, raise the roof for the Rock who saved us! Let's march into his presence singing praises, lifting the rafters with our hymns! And why? Because God is the best, High King over all the gods.

PSALM 95:1–3 MSG

Nothing is more beautiful than the sound of worship. It can leave us in tears or give us chill bumps as we recognize God's awesomeness. It has a powerful way of penetrating the deepest places in our soul, reminding us of God's unwavering love and kindness. The psalmist in today's verse offers demonstrative examples of raising the roof in gratitude. We're encouraged to shout praises. We're to march into His presence singing. And at the same time, we're to withhold nothing as we lay out our love and appreciation of the Lord. Friend, what does praise look like in your life? Does God feel gratitude from you? Be intentional with it. Let it be part of your prayers every day!

God, You have been so good to me. I see the ways You've shown up and blessed me. I recognize Your hand in every circumstance. Help me be quick to thank You for being alive and active in my life. In the name of Jesus. Amen.

When We Bow before Him

So come, let us worship: bow before him, on your knees before God, who made us! Oh yes, he's our God, and we're the people he pastures, the flock he feeds.

PSALM 95:6–7 MSG

Bowing before God is an act of worship because it recognizes Him as above us. Literally. It's a visual that packs a powerful punch, acknowledging the Lord's position as elevated in our heart and mind. And every time we take a knee, we show respect and honor to the One worthy of all praise. When we kneel in humility, let it remind us of times God made a significant impact on our life. Let it be a moment when we remember the ways He has made good on His promises. And let us praise Him for the awesome privilege of being His child and He, our God. Don't be legalistic about it. Don't think God only hears praise from those on bended knee. But when the time is right, bow down and let those praises pour forth.

God, I love You. I praise You for being magnificent. And I honor You by bowing down, grateful to be in the presence of the Most High King! In the name of Jesus. Amen.

Tell the World

Everyone everywhere, lift up your joyful shout to God!
Sing your songs tuned to his glory! Tell the world how
wonderful he is. For he's the awe-inspiring God, great and
glorious in power! We've never seen anything like him!
Mighty in miracles, you cause your enemies to tremble.
No wonder they all surrender and bow before you!

PSALM 66:1–3 TPT

Your testimony is a praise to God for His faithfulness. It's the story of how He intervened in your life to bring about freedom and restoration. It's a reminder of His promises fulfilled as well as hope for more to come. And it reveals the blessing that comes from a heart surrendered to the Lord's will and ways. What is your story, friend? What causes you to raise a hallelujah? Being saved from a bad situation? Seeing new opportunities come your way in business? Watching a dead relationship come back to life? Don't forget to tell the world how wonderful He is. Everyone needs hope to cling to!

God, I don't know how You pulled it off, but You did. I'm so thankful for Your mighty hand moving in my life. I simply could not make it through this life without You, and I'm going to tell the world all about it! In the name of Jesus. Amen.

Miracles Multiplied

Everyone will say, "Come and see the incredible things God has done; it will take your breath away! He multiplies miracles for his people!" He made a highway going right through the Red Sea as the Hebrews passed through on dry ground, exploding with joyous excitement over the miracles of God.

PSALM 66:5–6 TPT

When God split the Red Sea in two so the fleeing Israelites could continue their journey from slavery to freedom, there was no doubt it was a miracle. It was a big miracle indeed! Bodies of water don't split on their own. But then came the mini miracle of drying the seabed so His people wouldn't get stuck in mud and mire as they crossed. It was an added bonus, multiplying God's already amazing act of parting the sea. Friend, ask the Lord to give you spiritual eyes to see the mini miracles surrounding the big one. You don't want to miss any opportunities to praise God as He displays His faithfulness in extraordinary ways.

God, I appreciate that You are a God of miracles, looking for opportunities to multiply them as You bless Your people. Open my eyes so I can see You at work and glorify Your name! In the name of Jesus. Amen.

Let Everyone Know

Praise God, all you peoples. Praise him everywhere and let everyone know you love him!

PSALM 66:8 TPT

How would people know you love God? What does your life preach? It's important to remember that people watch how we live. They observe the way we handle the hard seasons of marriage and parenting. They look at how we hold up through grief and loss. They take note of how we react when we're feeling stressed out. Are we clinging to God for hope, or are we stuck in the pit? When the bad news hits, do we stand in the peace of Jesus, or do we complain constantly? One of the most powerful ways we can show others we love the Lord is to let our words and actions reveal we're trusting Him in the good times and the bad times. We can talk about our steadfast faith that God will come through. We can praise Him now for the details we know He is working out for our good. Let everyone know you love Him!

God, remind me that others are watching, and let my life always point to You in heaven! In the name of Jesus. Amen.

He Will Not Allow You to Stumble

Praise the One who gives us life and keeps us safe,
who does not allow us to stumble in the darkness.

PSALM 66:9 VOICE

Let's raise the roof to the One who won't allow us to stumble when we're blinded. It's easy to make mistakes when we can't see clearly, but scripture says God won't let it happen. Even when we're blindsided and caught off guard, the Lord will keep us steady because our faith is anchored in Him. He will keep us safe when life overwhelms and confuses. Where do you need to embrace this truth in your life right now? Did you just receive terrible news? Are you facing a scary health report from your doctor? Has someone made inappropriate advances toward you in the workplace? Are you walking through grief because you lost someone near and dear to you? These are the times you cling to God, knowing He will navigate you through them. You can praise Him for protecting you from stumbling. You are safe.

God, thank You for understanding how dark times can cause me to stumble and promising to keep me sheltered and out of harm's way. In the name of Jesus. Amen.

God Won't Refuse

Blessed be God, who didn't turn away when I was praying and didn't refuse me his kindness and love.

PSALM 66:20 TLB

As you read today's verse, can you feel the weight of gratitude in the writer's words? Can you hear the relief the psalmist experienced because God was there when he needed Him the most? Think back to a time when you felt this way. Was it through a long and painful divorce? Was it through a very personal tragedy? Maybe you had a tough season of life on all fronts. Regardless, you saw God show up in extraordinary ways and reveal His matchless love for you. When others turned their backs because they couldn't stand the heat, the Lord didn't. You saw His kindness play out in tangible ways. He never refused your cries for help. He didn't sit in judgment of your circumstances. Instead, God was right there beside you. Take a moment to praise Him for all He has done, and pour out your heart in gratitude for the way He embraced you at that critical moment.

God, I'm humbled by Your steadfast love. Hear my praises for the kindness and generosity You showed me. In the name of Jesus. Amen.

Let God Be Your Praise

You must treat foreigners with the same loving care—remember, you were once foreigners in Egypt. Reverently respect God, your God, serve him, hold tight to him, back up your promises with the authority of his name. He's your praise! He's your God! He did all these tremendous, these staggering things that you saw with your own eyes.

DEUTERONOMY 10:19–21 MSG

Sometimes we forget the amazing things God has done for us. We forget the miraculous ways He changed our circumstances and saved us from regret. We forget how He softened stone-cold hearts to seek reconciliation when it seemed impossible. We forget about the times the cash showed up, the decision was reversed, the phone call came, the job was offered, and the pregnancy test was finally positive. Let moments like these be reminders to shout your praises to the heavens! Allow these blessings to be why you hold tight to God through thick and thin. And be encouraged to continue serving Him daily with your life. It's because you feel His love so deeply that you are able to love others. Friend, let God be your praise!

God, I will raise a hallelujah, for You are good all the time! In the name of Jesus. Amen.

You Are Chosen and Faultless

Long ago, even before he made the world, God chose us to be his very own through what Christ would do for us; he decided then to make us holy in his eyes, without a single fault—we who stand before him covered with his love. His unchanging plan has always been to adopt us into his own family by sending Jesus Christ to die for us. And he did this because he wanted to!

EPHESIANS 1:4–5 TLB

Praise the Lord because you are chosen! Before He created the world and everything in it, God chose you to be His own. And because of the gift of the cross where His Son, Jesus, died for your sins, you are holy. Rather than dripping with sin, you are now covered with God's love. Because Jesus is your Savior and Lord, you are faultless before Him. If that's not reason enough to raise a hallelujah, what is? Praise God for His unchanging plan of adoption into His family. Worship Him for allowing His own Son to die in your place. And glorify the name of God because His heart for you is always good!

God, no one else is like You! In the name of Jesus. Amen.

God Delights in You

Moreover, because of what Christ has done, we have become gifts to God that he delights in, for as part of God's sovereign plan we were chosen from the beginning to be his, and all things happen just as he decided long ago.

EPHESIANS 1:11 TLB

The idea that God could actually delight in us is sometimes hard to believe. When we take inventory of our lives—considering the choices and decisions that make us feel ashamed—we struggle to embrace this idea as truth. We wonder if certain things we did slipped His gaze, because they did nothing to glorify God. Thinking through specific seasons of sinning, we feel certain it's just a matter of time before He reviews His notes and changes His mind. But when we entertain these kinds of thoughts, we're forgetting what Jesus did to take away our sins. His blood washed them all away—past, present, and future. So rather than sit in self-doubt, choose instead to praise God for loving you enough to make a way for your sins to be erased once and for all.

God, I am so thankful for Your plan for me to be with You forever. Let my life be worthy of Your delight! In the name of Jesus. Amen.

Praying for Others

I have never stopped thanking God for you. I pray for you constantly, asking God, the glorious Father of our Lord Jesus Christ, to give you wisdom to see clearly and really understand who Christ is and all that he has done for you.

EPHESIANS 1:16–17 TLB

What a privilege to pray for others. What an honor to take those we care about to the throne room in our time with God. He hears every word that's on our heart, spoken and unspoken. He understands the burden we carry for our family and friends. He sees the love we show to the lost and broken. God delights in our grateful heart that celebrates the community we've been given. And the Lord's ear is always tuned to our voice and ready to listen as we unpack what we're thinking and feeling. What a praiseworthy gift to be able to pray to God on behalf of others!

God, hear my prayers for those I care about. I praise You for encouraging me to include petitions and thanksgiving for others in my time with You. Thank You for hearing each request I bring on behalf of my friends and family. I trust You with them! In the name of Jesus. Amen.

Praising God Every Day

My heart explodes with praise to you! Now and forever my heart bows in worship to you, my King and my God! Every day I will lift up my praise to your name with praises that will last throughout eternity.

PSALM 145:1–2 TPT

King David vowed to praise the Lord every day. That was a bold declaration to make, let alone to document for the whole world to see! David essentially created a challenge not only for himself but also for others over generations to come. What if you decided to do the same? Are you up for the challenge? What if before your feet hit the floor in the morning, you shared with God what you're grateful for? And what if as you crawled into bed that night, you spent time thanking Him for all He did throughout the day? Think about how being watchful for the Lord's hand in your life might change your perspective during the day. Think about how it might improve your attitude. Let's choose to be women on the lookout for God's goodness in our lives, and then let's lift our voices in praise every time we see it!

God, please give me the spiritual eyes to see Your hand moving! In the name of Jesus. Amen.

There's No End to God

Lord, you are great and worthy of the highest praise! For there is no end to the discovery of the greatness that surrounds you. Generation after generation will declare more of your greatness and declare more of your glory.

PSALM 145:3–4 TPT

Let's raise a hallelujah to the God who has no end! Let's praise the One whose greatness can never be entirely discovered! Think about how disheartening it would be to get to the end of God. How uninspiring to have Him all figured out. How would we be able to place our complete faith in someone ordinary? Let's praise God for being shrouded in mystery and full of majesty. To each generation, His awesomeness is revealed through powerful testimony. There is always more to declare about His glory. Our God is magnificent and praiseworthy—let's raise our voices as we shout it throughout the earth! Let's share the news of His greatness boldly so it ripples to the next group of believers.

God, I deeply appreciate that You can't be dissected or unpacked. No one can fully understand who You are or how You work. Thank You for being extraordinary in every way! In the name of Jesus. Amen.

Waiting for a Breakthrough

Our hearts bubble over as we celebrate the fame of your marvelous beauty, bringing bliss to our hearts. We shout with ecstatic joy over your breakthrough for us. You're kind and tenderhearted to those who don't deserve it and very patient with people who fail you. Your love is like a flooding river overflowing its banks with kindness.

PSALM 145:7–8 TPT

We're all waiting for a breakthrough somewhere in our life. Each of us is desperate for the Lord's mercy to shine through once again. We are watching for redemption and restoration at God's hand. What about you, friend? Where are you asking God for a breakthrough? Maybe it's a health issue for you or someone you love. Maybe it's a financial issue, and you're at the end of your rope. Maybe it's a heart issue, and you can't muster the courage to forgive an offender. Regardless of the step forward you're waiting for, you can have faith God will bring it! So raise a hallelujah right now, for your deliverance is on its way, according to His will and timing!

God, my heart bubbles over with gratitude because of Your commitment to deliverance. I am ready for the breakthrough I've been asking for! In the name of Jesus. Amen.

God Sees the Broken Down

The Eternal sustains all who stumble on their way. For those
who are broken down, God is near. He raises them up in hope.
All eyes have turned toward You, waiting in expectation;
when they are hungry, You feed them right on time.

PSALM 145:14–15 VOICE

According to today's scripture, God is gentle when we feel broken. He doesn't leave us alone or roll His eyes in frustration. Instead, His heart is tender, and He's ready to support us as we navigate the heartbreak. Without our even having to ask, God comes very near and gives us a sense of peace and hope. He is an excellent Father who cares deeply for His children. That's why we can turn our eyes to the Lord in expectation. It's why we can trust He is already working out the details for our benefit. It's why we can glorify His name in the middle of the mess, for we know His plans for us are good.

God, I lift my eyes to You in praise and worship because I know You won't leave me in this tough place. You won't let me sit in my brokenness for long. In the name of Jesus. Amen.

Praying with Sincerity

The Eternal stays close to those who call on Him, those who pray sincerely. All of you who revere Him—God will satisfy your desires. He hears the cries for help, and He brings salvation. All of you who love God—He will watch out for you, but total destruction is around the corner for all the wicked.

PSALM 145:18–20 VOICE

Pray with a genuine heart when asking God for help. Don't state your request flippantly. Don't demand His response or action. Instead, be sure to pray with reverence to the only One who can truly save and restore your heart. When you love God and are submitted to His will and ways for your life, He will watch out for you. He will stick close to you. And He will bring deliverance. Let Him know right now where you're struggling and desperate for rescue. Be frank and authentic as you share what's heavy on your heart. And couple your prayer with a grateful spirit, because you can believe beyond a doubt that God will do right by you.

God, help my heart be right when I go to You in prayer. Keep me from praying insincere or superficial prayers. I know You will bring freedom from what binds me. In the name of Jesus. Amen.

Praising Him with Your Life

I will refuse to look on any sordid thing; I detest the worthless deeds of those who stray; evil will not get a hold on me. I will rid my heart of all perversion; I will not flirt with any evil.

PSALM 101:3–4 VOICE

You can praise God simply by living with great intention. When you pursue righteousness—not perfection—and make the often-hard choices to follow His will and ways, you are engaging in a beautiful act of worship. Saying no to the desires of the flesh and instead embracing His commands brings Him delight. Be careful not to sit in judgment or think of yourself as holier than others. Don't look down on those in seasons of struggle, because we all go through those seasons from time to time. Focus on your own life—your own choices and actions. Worry only about ridding your heart of sinful ways. Keep in check your fleshy flirtations with temptation. And remember that every decision you make to stand strong in faith translates to praise in God's eyes.

God, my desire is to glorify Your name through the way I live my life. I want You to be exalted through the choices I make. In the name of Jesus. Amen.

Drawing the Line

The one who makes a habit of deceit will not be welcome in my house; the one who lies will not remain in my presence for long. Every morning I will purge all the wicked from the land so as to rid the city of the Eternal of those who practice evil.

PSALM 101:7–8 VOICE

While God doesn't want our heart to be like a gated community, He does support drawing a line in the sand. We aren't to reject helping those who need it because their life is messier than ours. We shouldn't turn up our nose to people struggling in sin, thinking we're better than them. And we are called to have a servant's heart toward the "least of these." With the Lord's help, we can walk the tightrope of helping others without being pulled into their bad choices. And we can draw a line in the sand regarding what comes into our home or heart. These deliberate decisions will be like a fresh fragrance of praise to God.

God, let my bold choices praise You as I protect myself from falling into the sinful ways of those around me. In the name of Jesus. Amen.

Letting God Be

"I will hide in God, who is my rock and my refuge. He is my shield and my salvation, my refuge and high tower. Thank you, O my Savior, for saving me from all my enemies. I will call upon the Lord, who is worthy to be praised; he will save me from all my enemies."

2 SAMUEL 22:3–4 TLB

Let God be the place you hide away when you're hurting. Let Him be your shield. When you're scared, let Him be your refuge and high tower. As the walls begin to close in on you, let God be your rock and refuge. Be quick to ask Him for deliverance from whatever is coming against you, because scripture reinforces the truth that we serve a God who will save us. That is praiseworthy news! When you go to the Lord for help, do so with expectation, knowing He will act!

God, what a huge relief to know that no matter what I need, You will be that for me. From a Savior to a deliverer to a defender, You will meet me in my mess. I'm praising You for Your faithfulness and kindness toward those who love You. In the name of Jesus. Amen.

Hope in a Hostile World

A hostile world! I called to God, to my God I cried out. From his palace he heard me call; my cry brought me right into his presence—a private audience!

2 SAMUEL 22:7 MSG

No doubt about it—we live in a hostile world. Never mind what's happening globally or nationally, we experience this joy-draining hostility in our day-to-day life. We're battling on so many levels, aren't we? We're battling broken hearts as we watch our kids struggle. We're trying to feel good about who we are in a world that tells us we'll never be good enough. Our relationships are attacked on the regular, and countless financial fires require our attention. So let's praise God that when we cry out to Him, our weary voice floats up into the heavens and into His holy palace. He hears us every time. And at that moment, it's as if our voice is the only one that matters.

God, You always make me feel special, giving me Your undivided attention. Thank You for hearing me each time I call to You, granting me a private audience. I will exalt Your name and praise You every day. In the name of Jesus. Amen.

When We're Surprised to Be Loved

But me he caught—reached all the way from sky
to sea; he pulled me out of that ocean of hate,
that enemy chaos, the void in which I was drowning.
They hit me when I was down, but God stuck
by me. He stood me up on a wide-open field;
I stood there saved—surprised to be loved!

2 SAMUEL 22:17-20 MSG

Let's raise a hallelujah to the God who pulls us from enemy chaos and sets us in a wide-open field where we can catch our breath. When we're afraid of being pulled under by the weight of worry, God will reach down for us. No matter the situation, He promises to stick by us as we work through it. Anytime the Lord rescues us, we may find ourselves surprised by His amazing kindness and generosity. Friend, His love for you is endless and unfathomable. Take a moment to praise Him for being such an awesome God.

God, thank You for being willing to get in the mess with me. I may feel abandoned by others but never by You. Honestly, sometimes my heart is so full of gratitude for Your love and kindness it feels like it might burst! In the name of Jesus. Amen.

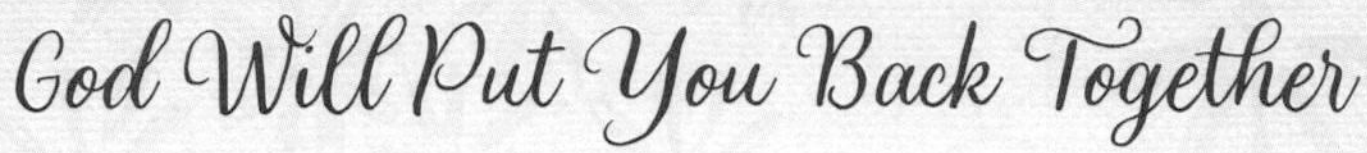

God Will Put You Back Together

I feel put back together, and I'm watching my step. God rewrote the text of my life when I opened the book of my heart to his eyes.

2 SAMUEL 22:24–25 MSG

When you look at your life, consider it a puzzle of many different-shaped pieces. There is a beautiful complexity to who you are. And while most of the time the pieces are securely in place, some seasons of life bring so much trauma and chaos that only God can put you back together again. In our desperation for wholeness, He is clearly our only hope. So let's glorify the Lord for His willingness to mend and restore. Let's praise Him for bringing unity to our body, mind, and soul so we can live in victory!

God, I don't know how You do it. I'm always amazed by Your generosity toward me over and over again. Today I lift up Your name above all, acknowledging the awesomeness of Your ways. Thank You for putting no limit on the number of times You put me back together again. I will forever shout Your praises to the world! In the name of Jesus. Amen.

When God Transforms a Heart

Now I, Nebuchadnezzar, praise and extol and honor the King of heaven, all of whose works are truth, and His ways justice. And those who walk in pride He is able to put down.

DANIEL 4:37 NKJV

If King Nebuchadnezzar could turn to God, then anyone can. He was a self-promoting, prideful ruler whose heart was miraculously changed. And in the end, he turned to the Lord and praised Him. Let's glorify God for having the power to transform even the hardest heart. Friend, is that your story? Did the Lord do a mighty work in your life? Or maybe you watched as He renovated the heart of someone you loved. Nothing and nobody can make those kinds of changes but God Himself. When you think of the far-reaching effects of the transformation He has wrought, no doubt you'll want to raise a hallelujah in deep gratitude.

God, thank You for having the power to make transformational changes in us. Thank You for helping us become who You created us to be. I give You all praise and honor, for You are magnificent! Keep me close and change me as You see fit. I trust You to work in the nooks and crannies of my life. In the name of Jesus. Amen.

Take Your Breath Away

Everything I am will praise and bless the Lord!
O Lord, my God, your greatness takes my breath away,
overwhelming me by your majesty, beauty, and splendor!

PSALM 104:1 TPT

What has God done to take your breath away? Where have you seen His greatness in your life? How has He overwhelmed you with His awesomeness? Maybe you've been miraculously healed from a terminal disease. Maybe your husband had a change of heart and decided to work things out instead of leave. Maybe your small business experienced an unexpected boom from a social media post. Maybe your family was able to work out their differences and reunite once again. Maybe your pregnancy test was positive after months of negatives. Friend, take heart and have hope. God is on the move, and His greatness is limitless. Praise Him for His wonderful works that have the power to both fill your heart and take your breath away. Rest in the truth that you are deeply loved.

God, I see You moving in my life and I give You the glory, for Your works and ways are wonderful! Everything I am will praise and bless You! In the name of Jesus. Amen.

His Kindness, Goodness, and Compassion

From your kindness you send the rain to water the mountains from the upper rooms of your palace. Your goodness brings forth fruit for all to enjoy. Your compassion brings the earth's harvest, feeding the hungry. You cause the grass to grow for livestock, along with the fruit, grains, and vegetables to feed mankind.

PSALM 104:13–14 TPT

Today's verses speak to the depth of care God shows us. If you've ever doubted that He sees you and your needs, revisit this passage of scripture; it will remind you of the Lord's kindness, goodness, and compassion. The truth is that He sees it all, every bit of lack and deficiency you're facing right now. He sees the fear rising up in your spirit. He sees where your insecurities are tangling you up. He recognizes the panic and stress. And just as He sends the rain, brings forth a harvest, and grows grass all to satisfy the needs of His children, God will sustain you in those desperate places too. Praise Him now for the bounty of goodness that's on its way!

God, I'm so grateful for Your promise of provision! In the name of Jesus. Amen.

Every Sweet Thought

I will sing my song to the Lord as long as I live!
Every day I will sing my praises to God. May you be
pleased with every sweet thought I have about you,
for you are the source of my joy and gladness.

PSALM 104:33–34 TPT

Do you reflect on the good things about God? Do you spend time meditating on who He is and all He has done? Friend, something powerful happens when we remember His goodness in our life. And ruminating over the ways God has rescued and restored is life giving because it offers us hope He will do it again. Why not build in extra time each day to consider the ways the Lord has blessed you? Sit with memories of His awesomeness. Unpack His fulfilled promises. And then raise a mighty hallelujah as you thank God for being favored in His sight. Let Him hear your voice break out in praise for His majesty!

God, hear my heart today as I reflect on Your goodness. Hear my sweet thoughts as I meditate on all You are to me. There is none like You in all the heavens and earth! In the name of Jesus. Amen.

Others Are Watching

Picture this: It's midnight. In the darkness of their cell, Paul and Silas—after surviving the severe beating—aren't moaning and groaning; they're praying and singing hymns to God. The prisoners in adjoining cells are wide awake, listening to them pray and sing.

ACTS 16:25 VOICE

Imagine the mighty testimony the other prisoners witnessed. Rather than wallow in self-pity, rant at God, or roll into a ball and cry, Paul and Silas prayed. They sang sweet hymns to the Lord in the darkness of night. And as much as the others may have wanted to sleep, they had no choice but to listen to their praise. Friend, it's important to realize others are watching to see how you navigate the ups and downs of life. They see how you respond to the hard moments. They take note of your reaction to hardship. That's why choosing to have a grateful heart for others to witness is an act of praise to God in heaven. Keep in mind that how you handle life preaches.

God, help me remember that others are watching how I respond to struggles and hardship. Give me a desire to praise You no matter what circumstances I'm facing. In the name of Jesus. Amen.

Everyone Everywhere

You answer our prayers with amazing wonders and with awe-inspiring displays of power. You are the righteous God who helps us like a father. Everyone everywhere looks to you, for you are the confidence of all the earth, even to the farthest islands of the sea.

PSALM 65:5 TPT

Don't think that if everyone everywhere is looking to God for help and hope you might get lost in the crowd. It just doesn't work that way. Somehow in His supernatural abilities, the Lord is able to give His full attention to every single person at the same time. That means you're not competing for His ear. You aren't jockeying for position and waiting in line. And even more, His power and majesty never run dry. Let's raise a hallelujah because our God doesn't have to compromise. We can pray to Him confidently, trusting He will meet every need every time.

God, I'm in awe of how wonderful You are. What a privilege to pray, knowing You turn Your full attention to me and hear the depth of my heart. How amazing to realize Your power and wonder can never be depleted. I praise You for being magnificent in every way! In the name of Jesus. Amen.

Startle and Stun

O God, to the farthest corners of the planet people will stand in awe, startled and stunned by your signs and wonders. Sunrise brilliance and sunset beauty both take turns singing their songs of joy to you.

PSALM 65:8 TPT

Praise God for both startling and stunning those who love Him. What a privilege to serve a God with the power to move a heart in such a way. Think back to a time when the Lord's provision caught you off guard. Remember a moment when His protection jolted you. Have you ever seen a swift move of God's kindness that knocked you to your knees? Can you recall being humbled by His healing power? Friend, lift your hands to heaven and thank God for His magnificence! Our Lord is willing and able to stun us with His love. Open your eyes to see His brilliance!

God, I love You and the beautiful way You delight those who call You Father. Thank You for being bigger and better than everything else in the universe. Thank You for leaving me awestruck by Your kindness and generosity. Hear my voice magnify Your name in all the earth! In the name of Jesus. Amen.

When Nature Praises God

Luxuriant green pastures boast of your bounty as you make every hillside blossom with joy. The grazing meadows are covered with flocks, and the fertile valleys are clothed with grain, each one dancing and shouting for joy, creation's celebration! They're all singing their songs of praise to you!

PSALM 65:12–13 TPT

Even the pastures, meadows, and valleys shine the Lord's goodness into the world. His own creation can't help but praise God with its brilliance. Take a moment to breathe in the beauty around you and raise a hallelujah to the One who thought it up and made it be. When we take a moment to drink in the splendor of nature, we'll be able to see His fingerprints everywhere. Do you feel closer to the Lord outdoors, taking in the rolling hills and countryside? Does a babbling brook connect to your spirit? Do snow-covered mountains leave you in awe of the Creator? Just as nature sings its songs of praise to God, join in the moment and celebrate His goodness!

God, I love those moments when nature connects my heart to Yours. I praise You for the beautiful world You have created. How magnificent! In the name of Jesus. Amen.

The Lord Protects His People

Oh, praise the Lord, for he has listened to my pleadings! He is my strength, my shield from every danger. I trusted in him, and he helped me. Joy rises in my heart until I burst out in songs of praise to him. The Lord protects his people and gives victory to his anointed king.

PSALM 28:6–8 TLB

The psalmist is celebrating that God listened when he pleaded and helped him work through his struggles. He is praising the Lord for protection from danger. Friend, how have you seen Him intervene in your life? Did God hear your cries and restore a broken marriage? Did He bring a new friendship? Did He connect you to the right set of doctors and treatments? Did He restore your hope and give you the courage you asked for? Let joy rise in your heart as you remember these beautiful moments, and burst out in praise to a God who protects His people!

God, thank You for the promise of Your protection! I will cling to it with hope and expectation of Your help, and I will praise Your name with fervor for the deliverance I know You will bring. In the name of Jesus. Amen.

Letting God Be Your Shepherd

Save your people whom you love, and bless your chosen ones. Be our shepherd leading us forward, forever carrying us in your arms!

PSALM 28:9 TPT

Ask the Lord to be your Shepherd. Let Him guide you through life, clearing the path for you to follow. Too often, we decide the best thing for us is to go our own way. We make choices based on feelings and emotions. And we end up being led by our own fleshly desires instead of God's plan for our next steps. Even if we're not living in intentional defiance, we're saying no to Him and missing out on His blessing. But when we instead press into the Lord, following our loving Shepherd's lead, our faith will be rewarded. And we will have countless reasons to raise a hallelujah as we stay close to the One who saves!

God, I confess the times I have turned my back on You and followed my own plans. I haven't always trusted Your ways over mine. Help me shift my thinking so I can be in Your will, staying in step with Your plan and reaping the benefits that come from obedience. In the name of Jesus. Amen.

Praising Wherever You Go

Wherever I go, I will thank you. All the nations will hear my praise songs to you. Your love is so extravagant, it reaches higher than the heavens! Your faithfulness is so astonishing, it stretches to the skies! Lord God, be exalted as you soar throughout the heavens. May your shining glory be seen high above all the earth!

PSALM 108:3–5 TPT

Be ready and willing to thank the Lord no matter where you are. Be it a movie theater, a ski slope, a corporate meeting, or the back of a mountain bike, don't let any moment pass without giving praise where praise is due. Some may choose not to because they think the only way to recognize God's goodness is to be demonstrative. And while that certainly is a great way to worship the Lord and acknowledge His sovereignty, it isn't the only way. Sometimes all we can do is whisper "Thank You." We may only have the space to close our eyes and speak to Him from the heart. God hears all our praises. . .and each one delights His heart.

God, give me the reminder and the courage to praise You in the moment. There's always a way to recognize Your goodness no matter where I am. In the name of Jesus. Amen.

Enjoyable Praise

It's so enjoyable to come before you with uncontainable praises spilling from our hearts! How we love to sing our praises over and over to you, to the matchless God, high and exalted over all! At each and every sunrise we will be thanking you for your kindness and your love. As the sun sets and all through the night, we will keep proclaiming, "You are so faithful!"

PSALM 92:1–2 TPT

Sometimes we stay reserved in our praises. Rather than let go of our inhibitions and release our uncontainable praises, we remain low key. We stay on the down low. Maybe we're insecure, worrying what others might think. Maybe we're not sure what's okay and what isn't. So rather than allow our worship to burst forth, we tuck it away. Let this be your challenge to praise like the psalmist. Sing! Dance! Shout! Tell God why you're raising such a rowdy hallelujah to the heavens. Let yourself be free and enjoy it!

God, what an honor to praise You with all my might.
I love being able to have a blast while I'm glorifying
Your awesomeness! In the name of Jesus. Amen.

His Divine Complexity

What mighty miracles and your power at work—just to name a few! Depths of purpose and layers of meaning saturate everything you do. Such amazing mysteries are found within every miracle that nearly everyone seems to miss. Those with no discernment can never really discover the deep and glorious secrets hidden in your ways.

PSALM 92:5–6 TPT

It's difficult for us to understand the depth and dimension of God. He is filled with mystery, and His works are intricately layered with powerful meaning we so often miss in the moment. We focus on the deliverance and don't think to look further to detect the rest of His goodness. God's miracles are perfectly timed to bring the greatest benefit to those who love Him, but usually we take them at face value. Scripture reveals that within these miracles are more mysteries waiting to be discovered. How incredible is that! Ask God to give you discernment to see the deeper meaning behind His ways. Don't be afraid to dig in. And praise the Lord for His divine complexity!

God, I appreciate Your complexity, and I'm excited to learn more about who You are and the ways You work. In the name of Jesus. Amen.

The Wicked Won't Win

It's true the wicked flourish, but only for a moment; they foolishly forget their destiny with death, that they will all one day be destroyed forevermore. But you, O Lord, are exalted forever in the highest place of endless glory, while your opponents, the workers of wickedness, will all perish, forever separated from you.

PSALM 92:7–9 TPT

Praise the Lord that any thriving enjoyed by the wicked will be short lived. We may feel frustrated when wicked people seem to be winning. So often they seem to enjoy fame and fortune while the faithful don't. They appear to flourish while those who love the Lord ride the struggle bus. So let this verse be reason to raise a hallelujah to God because He always wins. We can find peace knowing no one trumps the Almighty or those who place their trust in Him. The wicked will perish, and God will be exalted forever.

God, it does my heart good to remember no one will ever best You. You're unstoppable and unbeatable. While the wicked may feel superior for a spell, their prosperity will never last. Amen and hallelujah. In the name of Jesus. Amen.

He Delivers Victory

You've said that those lying in wait to pounce on me would be defeated, and now it's happened right in front of my eyes, and I've heard their cries of surrender! Yes! Look how you've made all your devoted lovers to flourish like palm trees, each one growing in victory, standing with strength!

PSALM 92:11–12 TPT

What an amazing God to deliver victory just as He promised. We never have to wonder if God will come through for us. We don't have to stress that things may not work out. And we don't have to hold back from praising the Lord through the storm because we know He will lead us safely to peace. Even more, when we cling to God as we face hardship, we will flourish and find victory and strength in His presence. Let's give glory to the One who will never leave us alone to wither under the weight of life. With God we win.

God, I lift up Your name in praise as I remember all the times You've saved me from the enemy. You've delivered me into victory regardless of my circumstances. Thank You for being such a loving and faithful Father. In the name of Jesus. Amen.

Beautiful Strength

Listen to them! With pleasure they still proclaim:
"You're so good! You're my beautiful strength!
You've never made a mistake with me."

PSALM 92:15 TPT

All praise to the Lord for being our beautiful strength. Think back in your life to when this declaration was true and real for you. When have you seen the Lord's goodness play out in your circumstances? Maybe He healed your heart in the wake of a painful loss. Maybe He gave you courage to stand up for yourself. Perhaps He gave you a new perspective that eased the heartache a bit. Or maybe God gave you the confidence to step out of your comfort zone in unexpected ways. Consider the truth that the Lord has never made a mistake with you. He has planned every step with great intention. Today, thank Him for being mighty in your life.

God, I can see the times when You were my strength. How beautiful! I'm so grateful to serve a loving God who wants to see me thrive, not merely survive. I am moved as I consider how involved You have been in my life and all the ways You have kept me steady. Today, I praise You! In the name of Jesus. Amen.

When You Feel Abandoned by God

God, God. . .my God! Why did you dump me miles from nowhere? Doubled up with pain, I call to God all the day long. No answer. Nothing. I keep at it all night, tossing and turning.

PSALM 22:1–2 MSG

You've probably experienced a time in your life when you felt abandoned by God. Your prayers seemed to bounce off the ceiling. Maybe you felt shut down by the Lord, like you were in a big time-out. Maybe in faith you prayed over and over but heard nothing in response. Chances are God's apparent silence left you anxious and frustrated, battling an overwhelming feeling of hopelessness. Friend, never forget the truth that God hears you. Having faith means we choose to trust His timing and will. And rather than sink into the pit of despair, why not praise Him instead, firmly believing help is on the way?

God, I confess the times I've been angry and frustrated with You because I felt abandoned. You didn't seem to hear me or want to help. Grow my faith so I know without a doubt You are in the middle with me, working things out for my benefit. I know I can trust You! In the name of Jesus. Amen.

Faith through the Generations

Still, You are holy; You make Your home on the praises of Israel. Our mothers and fathers trusted in You; they trusted, and You rescued them. They cried out to You for help and were spared; they trusted in You and were vindicated.

PSALM 22:3–5 VOICE

What a gift to experience the generational blessing of a faith-filled family. What an encouragement to see their belief trickle down the family tree to influence others. Our testimony is powerful, which is why we should be talking about the times and ways God has shown up in our life. We need to share the hard moments and the praises, because others need to hear of His goodness. So teach those around you to praise God for what He has done in the previous generations and what He is doing now. Let Him hear you glorify His name and give Him credit. And know that in doing so, you are helping to build faith in the next generation to come.

God, I can see Your faithfulness throughout the years. I see the many blessings that have been passed down from parent to child. I praise You for making it so. In the name of Jesus. Amen.

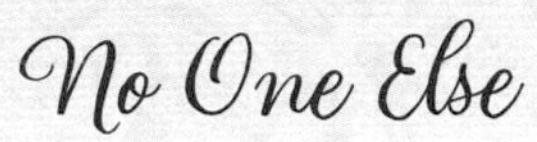

No One Else

Stay close to me—trouble is at my door;
no one else can help me.

PSALM 22:11 VOICE

You may be blessed with an amazing support system, but no one can help you like God can. Others may have the financial means to bail you out of trouble, but He owns the cattle on a thousand hills and has access to every asset. Your friends may have endless time to dedicate to helping you walk through the mess, but the Lord is in charge of determining time. And your family may love you fiercely and promise to support you no matter what, but only God can love without condition. Let's raise a hallelujah that there is no other above the Lord and that He takes care of every need, every time. Let's recognize that every good thing comes from Him. And let's thank Him for giving us amazing friends and family who are often His hands and feet in our life.

God, You think of everything. I feel so safe knowing You're in charge and fully engaged. Thank You for keeping me in Your sight and orchestrating the right help at the right time. In the name of Jesus. Amen.

The Amazing Creator

You are the Eternal, the only One. The skies are Your work alone—You made the heavens above those skies and the stars that fill them. You made the earth and everything upon it, the seas and all that lives within their depths. Your creation lives and is sustained by You, and those who dwell in the heavens fall down before You and worship.

NEHEMIAH 9:6 VOICE

Let's raise the roof as we praise the Lord for His amazing creation! To think He took a bunch of nothingness and formed the heavens and earth according to His master plan is purely overwhelming. The skies are above us because He made it so. Every star, every planet was placed there with great thought and intention. God shaped the earth, including everything upon it, and set it on its axis to rotate just so. The seas were His idea alone, and every living creature that swims in them, He made. Did you realize God was so thoughtful? Did you know He was so detailed and meticulous? Creation glorifies His name!

God, You are so very creative. I praise You as I consider all You've made for us to enjoy! In the name of Jesus. Amen.

Looking for God to Lead You

By day you led them with a Pillar of Cloud, and by night with a Pillar of Fire to show them the way they were to travel.

NEHEMIAH 9:12 MSG

If you look for the Lord, you will find Him. He doesn't try to conceal Himself. Your faith in God isn't a game of hide-and-seek. And when you're needing His leadership, remember that just as He led the Israelites out of Egypt, He will lead you out of your bondage too. You may not see Him with your eyes like they did, but your spirit will follow His as you navigate the mountaintops and valleys with the Lord. He will show you the way to go because His plans for you are always laced with hope. He wants you to thrive in His goodness. So be quick to raise a hallelujah every time you see God's hand leading you.

God, would You give me the spiritual eyes to see You? Sometimes I get lost or confused and I'm not sure which way to go. I don't see the path in front of me, and I'm pulled in too many directions. I'm trusting You to reveal my next step and walk with me as I journey. In the name of Jesus. Amen.

Maintained and Sustained

"You sent your good Spirit to instruct them, and you did not stop giving them bread from heaven or water for their thirst. For forty years you sustained them in the wilderness; they lacked nothing in all that time. Their clothes didn't wear out, and their feet didn't swell!"

NEHEMIAH 9:20–21 TLB

Did you catch it? For forty years, God kept their clothes from wearing out. No holes. No fraying. No rips or tears. The clothes they left Egypt with were the same clothes they wore as they walked into the Promised Land. Aside from the fact they were probably a tad out of style, they were well dressed. Even more, their feet—the only mode of transportation they had—never swelled. God maintained everything His chosen people needed for the journey. Friend, praise God right here and now because He is sustaining you too. Now that you're looking, where do you see it?

God, when I look at my life, I can see the places where You are keeping me safe and secure. I see where You have provided for my every need. And today, I am lifting my eyes to You in gratitude! Thank You for loving me in tangible ways. In the name of Jesus. Amen.

Singing a New Song

So make up a song like none other. Sing a new song to the Eternal. And let His praise echo clear across the earth. Let those who go to sea set sail with praise in the air. Let those who live along the waters' edge sing His praise.

ISAIAH 42:10 VOICE

Consider that when this verse suggests singing a new song of praise to God, it could mean choosing to change things up. It's easy for our prayer life to become stagnant and predictable. We use the same words to ask for the same things in the same way. So how might it reignite your passion for prayer and breathe new life into your relationship with God if you took a moment to let a new song of praise come forth? Everything needs refreshing from time to time, even the way we connect with the Lord. Ask Him to help you find fresh ways to praise and glorify His presence in your life.

God, I never want my praises to become robotic or mundane. I don't want my prayer life to be dull or ineffective. Help me find new ways to connect with You through worship. In the name of Jesus. Amen.

When Praise Is a Weapon

God's high and holy praises fill their mouths, for their shouted praises are their weapons of war! These warring weapons will bring vengeance on the nations and every resistant power—to bind kings with chains and rulers with iron shackles. Praise-filled warriors will enforce the judgment decreed against their enemies. This is the honor he gives to all his godly lovers. Hallelujah! Praise the Lord!

PSALM 149:6–9 TPT

Have you ever considered your praise to be a weapon of war? Scripture says praise can exact vengeance on enemy nations, but when you bring it down to a personal level, your praises can break the enemy's foothold in your life. It's difficult to be stuck in the pit of despair when you're busy telling God how wonderful He is. You can't live oppressed when your heart is full of gratitude. So when your heart is weighed down by parenting challenges, marriage struggles, financial worries, relationship troubles, fear, or grief, become a praise-filled warrior and raise a hallelujah to the Lord! Then watch how the enemy is defeated.

God, even when I feel overwhelmed and underwater, I always have reasons to praise You! Let praise be my weapon of choice. In the name of Jesus. Amen.

God Is the Expert

Don't put your life in the hands of experts who know nothing of life, of salvation life. Mere humans don't have what it takes; when they die, their projects die with them. Instead, get help from the God of Jacob, put your hope in God and know real blessing!

PSALM 146:3–5 MSG

Praise God for being the expert in your life! He knows exactly what needs to happen for you to live the life planned for you. Because He's sovereign, God knows what needs to happen next so your hope and joy are restored. He understands how you'll respond to difficult circumstances and knows the right moment to overwhelm you with His peace. The problem is that too often we expect well-meaning people to lead us. We look to them as experts. And while they may have the best of intentions, we should never put them in place of God. Raise your voice in thanks to a God who understands you better than any-one else and whose help will deliver a real blessing!

God, I'm so glad You know the ins and outs of me in such detail. I will trust You above everyone else. In the name of Jesus. Amen.

Trusting His Promises

He always does what he says—he defends the wronged, he feeds the hungry. GOD frees prisoners—he gives sight to the blind, he lifts up the fallen. GOD loves good people, protects strangers, takes the side of orphans and widows, but makes short work of the wicked.

PSALM 146:7–9 MSG

This you can take to the bank: God does what He says He will do. No ifs, ands, or buts about it. The Lord is faithful to His word. He is trustworthy to the end. Let this truth cause praise to erupt from deep in your spirit! Every promise God has made to you will come to pass. Has He promised to restore, renew, rescue, or release? Has He promised to undo or uncover? Maybe His promise is to bring hope, healing, or honor? Hold tight to what the Lord is pledging to do. Don't let your expectations wane. Because, friend, God always does what He says He will do, and that promise holds true for you!

God, give me the courage to hold on to what I believe You are promising. I don't want to fall prey to doubt or give up when our time frames don't align. Help me trust Your faithfulness to follow through. In the name of Jesus. Amen.

He Is Intimately Aware

You perceive every movement of my heart and soul, and you understand my every thought before it even enters my mind. You are so intimately aware of me, Lord. You read my heart like an open book and you know all the words I'm about to speak before I even start a sentence! You know every step I will take before my journey even begins.

PSALM 139:2–4 TPT

What does it do for your heart to know God is intimately aware of you? If you're like most women, you long to be known. Praise God for understanding the complexity of your heart! Never forget that you are fully seen, fully known, and fully loved by a God who is crazy about you. He understands your heart and soul as well as every thought that forms in your mind. He even knows the words being formulated before they pass through your lips. God knows well before you do every step you will take each day. Amazing, yes? Take a moment to show your gratitude to the One who knows you through and through and finds you spectacular!

God, thank You for caring enough to know everything about me. And thank You for loving me no matter what! In the name of Jesus. Amen.

He Planned Your Future

You've gone into my future to prepare the way, and in kindness you follow behind me to spare me from the harm of my past. You have laid your hand on me! This is just too wonderful, deep, and incomprehensible! Your understanding of me brings me wonder and strength.

PSALM 139:5–6 TPT

Let it be a point of praise that God has gone into the future and cleared a way for you. Friend, you are alive on earth right now for a reason. While you may not always feel it, you have purpose. Your presence means something! God planned long ago the exact time you'd come onto the kingdom calendar because He knew the gifts and talents He was implanting in you would be needed. Yes, you were planned with great intention! This powerful truth is something to celebrate! Don't brush it off or ignore it. Instead, ask the Lord to help you open your eyes to His plans for your future and embrace them. Ask Him to guide your steps to keep you walking toward them. And know that when you do, He will be glorified!

God, help me walk out my future with hope and purpose. In the name of Jesus. Amen.

You Can't Escape God

Where could I go from your Spirit? Where could I run and hide from your face? If I go up to heaven, you're there! If I go down to the realm of the dead, you're there too! If I fly with wings into the shining dawn, you're there! If I fly into the radiant sunset, you're there waiting!

PSALM 139:7–9 TPT

You can never escape God's love and care. Even when you want to hide in shame or guilt, it's impossible. No matter where you go, the Lord is there. Let this be reason enough to raise your voice in praise, because it means you are always under His loving eye. His help is available at all times. When you need to vent in frustration, cry out in pain, be held in your brokenness, scream in anger, grieve in loss, or gain perspective in your confusion, God is already right there ready for it all. There is no one else like Him! Even your closest family members and friends can't always be what you need right when you need it. Only God can. So praise Him today for choosing to be close at all times. Thank Him for loving you with no conditions.

God, what a comfort to know You are with me always. In the name of Jesus. Amen.

You're Mysteriously Complex

You formed my innermost being, shaping my delicate inside and my intricate outside, and wove them all together in my mother's womb. I thank you, God, for making me so mysteriously complex! Everything you do is marvelously breathtaking. It simply amazes me to think about it! How thoroughly you know me, Lord!

PSALM 139:13–14 TPT

Consider that there are glorious complexities about you that you're not even aware of. God made you with beautiful and intricate details only He fully understands. As a matter of fact, scripture says He was the One to form you in your mother's womb. He shaped you both inside and out. Friend, that means He decided everything about you before you took your first gulp of air. Praise God for being so involved in creating you to be the person He planned for you to be. And while you may struggle with the way you look or some of your characteristics, He doesn't. It's all by design, and He delights in you without fail! Trust that God made you the way He did on purpose, and embrace His decision and thank Him. Praise God you were made on purpose and for a purpose!

God, thank You for forming and shaping me! In the name of Jesus. Amen.

Your Days Are Numbered

You saw who you created me to be before I became me! Before I'd ever seen the light of day, the number of days you planned for me were already recorded in your book.

PSALM 139:16 TPT

How do you feel knowing God is fully aware of the exact number of days you have on planet Earth? Does that insight creep you out? Or does it fill you with a sense of gratitude that He is always in control? Let it be a gift to settle your heart and give you a profound sense of peace. Recognize it means you are cared for and loved by the One who created you. When He thought you up and chose your talents and giftings, God also knew when your work on earth would be done. In that moment, He decided when He would be ready to call you home into His presence. The number of your days has been set in stone since before He formed the world and everything in it. You are God's special creation and have an important role to play on earth. And then you will be welcomed home with open arms at His designated time.

God, thank You for knowing everything about me and my life. In the name of Jesus. Amen.

Every Single Moment

Every single moment you are thinking of me! How precious and wonderful to consider that you cherish me constantly in your every thought! O God, your desires toward me are more than the grains of sand on every shore! When I awake each morning, you're still with me.

PSALM 139:17–18 TPT

It's hard to understand how God could be thinking of us every single moment. And it's not just you He's thinking of but everyone! And everything! The Lord—in His awesomeness—is able to keep you at the forefront of His mind regardless of everything else He's doing and thinking. We struggle to remember everything we need at the grocery store. We forget to sign field trip permission slips. We miss payment due dates for bills, forget to send birthday cards, overlook emails that need our attention, and fail to recall details from important conversations. Let's raise a hallelujah that our God, the One we love, never accidentally ignores or overlooks anything to do with us. He's never caught off guard because His attention is elsewhere. What a blessing!

God, thank You for never being reckless or uninterested in my life. Thank You for keeping me on Your mind. In the name of Jesus. Amen.

He Will Search and Examine

God, I invite your searching gaze into my heart. Examine me through and through; find out everything that may be hidden within me. Put me to the test and sift through all my anxious cares. See if there is any path of pain I'm walking on, and lead me back to your glorious, everlasting way—the path that brings me back to you.

PSALM 139:23–24 TPT

You have access to healing by asking God to reveal any path of pain you may be walking in real time. Sometimes you're headed right toward destruction and don't even know it. You don't realize your well-intentioned choices are leading you astray. And when you're blinded by despair or desperation, you don't always make the wisest decisions. What a blessing to be able to let God search and examine you for potential trip-up situations. What a loving God to open your eyes to the tricky places that can cause trouble. Friend, never forget He is the only One who can lead you back to His will. He is the only One who can restore a broken heart and redirect you to greener pastures. God is always for you, and He is worthy of your praise for keeping you aligned with His plan for your life.

God, please search me and examine me.
I trust You. In the name of Jesus. Amen.

Faithful to His Promises

Praise the Eternal, all nations. Raise your voices, all people. For His unfailing love is great, and it is intended for us, and His faithfulness to His promises knows no end. Praise the Eternal!

PSALM 117:1–2 VOICE

Friend, take inventory of where God has been faithful to His promises in your life. How has God come through for you, doing what He said He would do? Being able to access this list quickly is important, because there will come a time when we'll need to remember God's goodness right then and there. It will be what offers hope. Like when we get the phone call from the doctor, and the news is terrifying. Or when our child endures a trauma, and we're struggling to wrap our mind around it. Or when our husband's secret life is revealed, and we're left speechless. In moments like these, remembering what God has done before gives us the power to praise Him for what He will do.

God, will You please bring to mind the times You've been faithful to me? I don't want to forget any of them because I know they will allow me to praise You in the storm. In the name of Jesus. Amen.

Why Do You Fear?

The LORD is my light and my salvation; whom shall I fear? The LORD is the strength of my life; of whom shall I be afraid?

PSALM 27:1 NKJV

God is very clear in the Bible that we should not be afraid of what comes our way. As a matter of fact, He instructs us to have no fear about 365 times in its pages! The whole idea is that if God is for us, we have nothing to fear. If He is the One we trust to guide us, we don't have to be scared. Since the Lord is our strength who infuses us with courage, we don't have to be trapped in worry. Let's celebrate this powerful truth! Let's ask God for the courage to walk in it so we don't have to live afraid. Yes, we will face alarming situations. We will have no choice but to navigate daunting moments. But praise the Lord for making sure we don't have to do it entangled in fear.

God, give me the confidence to be brave in You as I face fearful times throughout my life. Help me walk out Your command to be courageous. In the name of Jesus. Amen.

Dwelling in the House of the Lord

One thing I have desired of the Lord, that will I seek: that I may dwell in the house of the Lord all the days of my life, to behold the beauty of the Lord, and to inquire in His temple. For in the time of trouble He shall hide me in His pavilion; in the secret place of His tabernacle He shall hide me; He shall set me high upon a rock.

PSALM 27:4–5 NKJV

If you have received Jesus as your personal Savior, you no doubt realize it means you will dwell in the house of the Lord. When you close your eyes for the last time here on earth, they will open next to see His face. Your last exhale here will lead to your first inhale in the heavens. Just as the psalmist writes, let your eternal home with the Lord be what you desire most. Let the hope of eternity with Jesus power your praise, knowing that no matter what this crazy life brings, your salvation is secured. Friend, what a blessing to spend forever in the presence of God.

God, I'm excited to see You face-to-face and be in Your presence for eternity! In the name of Jesus. Amen.

A Standing Invitation

I heard your voice in my heart say, "Come, seek my face;" my inner being responded, "Yahweh, I'm seeking your face with all my heart." So don't turn your face away from me. You're the God of my salvation; how can you reject your servant in anger? You've been my only hope, so don't forsake me now when I need you!

PSALM 27:8–9 TPT

Let's raise a hallelujah because our amazing God has given us an open invitation to seek Him. Sometimes we think our mess is too much for God to handle. We worry that our season of sinning makes us too unholy for such a holy God. And rather than take Him up on His invitation to ask for help, we try to fix things our way. We may even decide without evidence that the Lord has rejected or abandoned us, but it's simply not true. Listen for His voice telling you to seek Him. And then seek Him with your whole heart.

God, I praise You for the standing invitation You've extended to me. What a blessing to know I can seek You at any time and for anything. You are so good all the time. In the name of Jesus. Amen.

God Fills the Gap

My father and mother abandoned me. But you,
Yahweh, took me in and made me yours.

PSALM 27:10 TPT

If you have no relationship with your parents, let this verse wash over you. If your relationship is broken and you've been rejected or abandoned by one or both of your parents, take heart that your heavenly Father will never leave you. The truth is, sometimes our earthly relationships crumble. We fall out of step with those we love. We watch them walk away, citing irreconcilable differences. And we suffer a heartbreak we never saw coming. What a blessing to know God steps in. He fills the gap and makes up the difference left by our parents. God's love reminds us we belong. Praise Him for making sure you are cared for! He thinks of everything.

God, thank You for knowing my need to feel like I belong. Thank You for knowing the longing in my heart to feel loved. I'm clinging to You as my Father, knowing You'll fill every gap my parents have left in my life. I'm trusting in You to remind me I matter. In the name of Jesus. Amen.

The Illuminated Path

O Eternal, show me Your way, shine Your light brightly on this path, and make it level for me, for my enemies are lurking in the recesses and ravines along the way.

PSALM 27:11 VOICE

When you feel lost and confused, praise the Lord for His willingness to illuminate the path He wants you to follow. Uncertainty about what should come next can be a horrible, destabilizing feeling, especially when you're usually sure of what to do. How wonderful, then, that God will open our eyes and reveal the path forward. Where do you need His guidance right now? What forked roads are before you? Are you tangled in insecurity, unable to see the plan He has laid out? Our God is a God of order, so when you ask for wisdom and discernment, He will most certainly give them. Hallelujah! Our Lord is faithful in every way.

God, show me Your way so I don't stumble in the dark. Make known the plans You have for my life. And give me the courage to take the next step with You even when I feel unsure in my flesh. I trust You. In the name of Jesus. Amen.

Waiting in Expectation

Please answer me: Don't give up. Wait for the Eternal in expectation, and be strong. Again, wait for the Eternal.

PSALM 27:14 VOICE

What does it mean to wait in expectation? It's actually a difficult choice we must make, and it takes a lot of faith to walk out. When we're in the middle between the ask and the answer, we're in dangerous territory. This is where our thoughts can trick us into believing God isn't listening. We decide we aren't important enough to get His attention. So choosing to wait in expectation means we rise above those thoughts and dig deep into our faith. We trust what His Word says about His faithfulness. And we praise Him in the waiting because we know the answer is on the way. It's a hard place to stand, but when we do, we'll reap the reward that comes from believing.

God, it feels unnatural for me to find peace in waiting. I'm so used to doing things myself that sometimes it takes all I have to wait on You. But Your works are wonderful, and it's in the waiting that I'm blessed. Please give me courage to stand strong in faith until Your perfect response arrives. In the name of Jesus. Amen.

A Majestic Makeover

As for those who grieve over Zion, God has sent me to give them a beautiful crown in exchange for ashes, to anoint them with gladness instead of sorrow, to wrap them in victory, joy, and praise instead of depression and sadness. People will call them magnificent, like great towering trees standing for what is right. They stand to the glory of the Eternal who planted them.

ISAIAH 61:3 VOICE

What an awesome God who promises to take the ashes of our life and exchange them for a beautiful crown. Only He can take something ugly and re-create it into something worthy. He is the One who can turn our sadness into joy. Nothing else can transform our sorrow and sadness into glee and gladness but the power of the Lord. Let's praise Him for not leaving us in our mess but instead blessing those who love Him with a majestic makeover!

God, take every pile of ashes and change them into something of value. Renovate the painful places into a weighty testimony of Your goodness in my life. I'm trusting You to exchange the messes I've made for something beautiful as I stand and praise Your hand at work. In the name of Jesus. Amen.

For a Very Special Purpose

The Spirit of the Lord, the Eternal, is on me. The Lord has appointed me for a special purpose. He has anointed me to bring good news to the poor. He has sent me to repair broken hearts, and to declare to those who are held captive and bound in prison, "Be free from your imprisonment!"

ISAIAH 61:1 VOICE

You've been appointed by the Lord for a very special purpose. As a matter of fact, it's something He planned specifically for you a long time ago. And rather than let it intimidate you or trigger insecurities, raise a hallelujah to the God who has had you on His mind since he beginning. What is your purpose? Ask Him to reveal it to you. Listen and look for His plan to unfold. Be ready to take a step of obedience as you trust God's will. And be excited because you've been chosen and anointed.

God, thank You for making me special. Thank You for choosing me for a specific purpose. I am humbled and honored by the anointing on my life, and I say yes to whatever You've planned for me. In the name of Jesus. Amen.

Let Praises Sprout Up

The whole earth sprouts newness and life in the springtime, and green shoots break through the well-seeded garden soil. That's what it is like with the Eternal's victory—the Lord will cause justice and praise to sprout up before all the nations, for all peoples to see.

ISAIAH 61:11 VOICE

When your heart is well seeded with faith in the Lord's sovereignty, every move of God's hand in your life will cause praise to sprout up. Scripture likens this to springtime. If we've planted in fertile soil and tended the garden regularly, new life will pop through the dirt without reminders. We don't have to force it. We don't have to cross our fingers and hope it happens. And when we invest in our relationship with God daily, our praises will erupt as a result. Our responses will glorify His name in all the earth simply because we choose to believe. Are you sowing seeds of faith in your life right now?

God, remind me of the value that comes from sowing seeds of faith. I want praises to sprout up from the time I invest in my relationship with You. In the name of Jesus. Amen.

What Do You Need?

There is only one strong, safe, and secure place for me; it's in God alone who gives me strength for the battle. He's my shelter of love and my fortress of faith, who wraps himself around me as a secure shield. I hide myself in this one who subdues enemies before me.

PSALM 144:1–2 TPT

No matter what you need, God has every answer. Do you need Him to be strong? Done. Need Him to be a safe place? No problem. Are you desperate for strength to get through a hard season of life? God will provide. Maybe you're looking to be encompassed in love and compassion. If so, the Lord is ready and waiting. Do you need an extra measure of faith? God will give it. Are you hoping to be surrounded on every side with a sense of security? Just ask Him. Maybe you want to be tucked away in God's peace until the storm passes. Friend, it's available. Praise the Lord for being what we need when we need it. All you have to do is tell Him what you need.

God, thank You for being my everything! I will exalt Your name to all who will listen! In the name of Jesus. Amen.

The God Who Notices

Lord, what is it about us that you would even notice us? Why do you even bother with us? For man is nothing but a faint whisper, a mere breath.

PSALM 144:3–4 TPT

Sometimes we have a powerful aha moment as we realize God cares about us. We're awestruck knowing we really do matter and are worthy in His eyes. To think the God of creation stoops down from His throne in heaven to meet with us here on earth can be overwhelming. This all-powerful and all-knowing King chooses to be in community with all-flawed and all-messy mankind. . .and we're forever grateful. What a praiseworthy God we get to be in relationship with—One who is sincerely delighted by His creation. Be encouraged, knowing the Lord not only notices you but draws even closer because of your faith. Hallelujah, He wants to be with you!

God, I'm amazed You notice and care for me, especially knowing the mess I sometimes make of my life. I wonder how a holy God can stand to be around someone who is not. But then I remember Jesus and His act of love on the cross, and my heart is full of praise once again. In the name of Jesus. Amen.

The Harp in Your Heart

My God, I will sing you a brand-new song! The harp inside my heart will make music to you! I will sing of you, the one who gives victory to kings—the one who rescues David, your loving servant, from the fatal sword.

PSALM 144:9–10 TPT

What a beautiful visual to imagine there is a harp in our heart that creates music to the Lord. Out of a deep sense of gratitude, our spirit lifts up praises to the One who moves us. Our soul celebrates the victory given to us by God, and we can't help but raise a hallelujah to the heavens. Our hands and voice reach toward the One who rescues and revives us through His love. And our praises are melodic to God's ears, delighting Him. Friend, what has the Lord done that causes the harp in your heart to make music in response?

God, I am moved by Your goodness. I'm touched by Your kindness. Thank You for bringing victory and healing to my circumstances, for You're the One who gets the glory. You alone cause the harp in my heart to make music. Let it glorify You in the heavens every time! In the name of Jesus. Amen.

Divine Abundance

Our barns will be filled to the brim, overflowing with the fruits of our harvest. Our fields will be full of sheep and cattle, too many to count, and our livestock will not miscarry their young. Our enemies will not invade our land, and there'll be no breach in our walls. What bliss we experience when these blessings fall! The people who love and serve our God will be happy indeed!

PSALM 144:13–15 TPT

Praise the Lord we have a Father who loves to bless us! He longs to fill our lives to the brim with His goodness. He wants our hearts to overflow with His love. He wants us to feel protected, safe, and secure because of His presence. God's plan is to bless us with abundance through our faith in Him. And when we experience these blessings, joy bubbles up and saturates our lives. The Lord is so very kind and generous to those who love Him. Thank Him right now for it!

God, I am so blessed to have You as my heavenly Father. I am so grateful for Your unfailing love and care. I bless You as You bless me. You are my favorite! In the name of Jesus. Amen.

The God of Forever

God, your name is eternal, God,
you'll never be out-of-date.

PSALM 135:13 MSG

What a relief to know God will never be out of date, especially considering we live in a world where everything expires. Nothing here on earth will stand the test of time. Relationships will end. Jobs will come to a close. Family dynamics will change. Even your body will feel the effects of time and eventually give out. That's why it's important we cling to the powerful truth that the Lord is eternal. He is unstoppable. He is timeless. And when we choose to place our faith in Him, it's good for the long haul. We can rest knowing the buzzer won't go off signaling the end of His wisdom or love or help. No, God is trustworthy forever!

God, You are hard to wrap my brain around. Your awesomeness is too much for me to process. I'm so grateful Your thoughts are higher than mine and Your ways are better. I'm so glad I cannot figure You out. And I love that while everything else will eventually come to an end, You never will. You're a timeless treasure! In the name of Jesus. Amen.

He Will Clear Your Name

Clear my name, God; stick up for me against these loveless, immoral people. Get me out of here, away from these lying degenerates. I counted on you, God. Why did you walk out on me? Why am I pacing the floor, wringing my hands over these outrageous people?

PSALM 43:1–2 MSG

When you need Him to, trust that God will stick up for you. He will delight in defending you, His beloved. When you're feeling hard pressed on every side, He will gladly rescue you from the mounting pressure to conform. The Lord will clear your name, protecting your reputation from harm and hatred. The truth is that sometimes our circumstances look bleak. They feel overwhelming on every level. And sometimes we blame God. But praise the Lord for staying faithful to His promise to save. He won't let us down or leave us to rot. So take heart and trust that He will clear your name!

God, what good news to know You promise to protect my name from those bent on hurting me. Even when I can't see You at work, I know what Your Word says. By faith, I am choosing to believe. In the name of Jesus. Amen.

When We Want to Throw a Pity Party

Why are you down in the dumps, dear soul? Why are you crying the blues? Fix my eyes on God—soon I'll be praising again. He puts a smile on my face. He's my God.

PSALM 43:5 MSG

Sometimes it's fun to throw a pity party for ourselves. Sometimes we're so overwhelmed by the hard parts of life that we just can't help but give in to despair. Rather than stand in faith and ask the Lord to fill us with hope, we curl up in a ball and wave the white flag. We've all done this. Can you remember the last time you did? The next time you want to feel sorry for yourself, be deliberate to raise a hallelujah instead. Rather than focusing on all that is difficult, recount how God has saved you in the past. Fix your eyes on the Lord—doing so will help restore your praise response to His goodness.

God, sometimes I do love a good pity party. Thanks for the reminder that despair is not Your plan for me. Instead, I will find hope and a reason to praise You by simply keeping my eyes fixed on Your promises. In the name of Jesus. Amen.

God's Love Never Quits

Give thanks to God—he is good and his love never quits. Say, "Save us, Savior God, round us up and get us out of these godless places, so we can give thanks to your holy Name, and bask in your life of praise." Blessed be God, the God of Israel, from everlasting to everlasting. Then everybody said, "Yes! Amen!" and "Praise God!"

1 CHRONICLES 16:34-36 MSG

Love can be so tricky, don't you think? In so many situations, it doesn't seem to stick. People are fickle about it. Think of all the times you've fallen in and out of love in your life. It's often conditional, strictly based on performance. You follow the rules, you receive love. But when you fail to do the right things, love fades. Our attempts to hold on to it from another can be frustrating and destabilizing, yet sometimes we go to extraordinary measures to try to keep it. Friend, what a blessing to know God's love for you will never quit. There is nothing you can do to make Him love you more or less than He does in this moment. Now that's praiseworthy!

God, thank You for giving love that's unconditional. In the name of Jesus. Amen.

Bigger and Better

Never doubt God's mighty power to work in you and accomplish all this. He will achieve infinitely more than your greatest request, your most unbelievable dream, and exceed your wildest imagination! He will outdo them all, for his miraculous power constantly energizes you.

EPHESIANS 3:20 TPT

Dream big, friend. Right now, think of the best life you can imagine for yourself. If the sky is the limit, what would you be doing? Where would you be living? What would your family life look like? Add in the goals you hope to accomplish in your career and personal life. Go big! Daydream about your most unbelievable desires for the future. Don't hold back! Envision the biggest and best life you can hope for, full of every good thing you can think of. Got it? Now realize scripture says God will achieve infinitely more than that. He will outdo it all. Praise God for His desire to trump our dreams with His perfect will for our life. Buckle up!

God, how exciting to know Your plans for my life are bigger and better than anything I can come up with! Thank You for creating a beautiful life of faith! In the name of Jesus. Amen.

Our Strong and Powerful God

You are feared; yes, You. And who can stand before
You when Your anger flares? You decreed judgment
from the heavens. The earth heard it and was petrified
with fear, completely still, when the True God arose
for judgment to deliver all the meek of the earth.

PSALM 76:7–9 VOICE

What a blessing that we serve a strong and powerful God who demands respect by simply existing! He isn't weak or wimpy. He can't be overrun, outsmarted, or outdone. And He doesn't back down to anyone. God can walk that tension between loving-kindness and righteous anger with perfection. He is the One who will judge the guilty with sharp precision, being fair and just at the same time. And when He speaks, the whole earth will listen and understand. God is everything we'd hope for in a Father and so much more. Praise Him for always showing His strength and tenderness at the right time.

God, I love knowing there is none like You in all the heavens and earth. I am so grateful there is no one above or beside You. Your strength is beautiful to me, and I praise You for being the amazing Father You are! In the name of Jesus. Amen.

Go to God for Mercy

Show mercy to me, O God, because people are crushing me—grinding me down like dirt underfoot—all day long. No matter what I do, I can't get myself out from under them. My enemies are crushing me, yes all day long, O Highest of High, for many come proud and raise their hands against me.

PSALM 56:1–2 VOICE

When you're craving compassion and kindness, let God be your source, not those around you. When life feels too big to navigate and you're weary and worried, ask the Lord to show His understanding. Every time you feel crushed by those who oppose you, let the Lord know you need His blessing as an encouragement to stand strong. It's common to ask friends and family to support us in difficult times. Hasn't the Lord given us some amazing people to go to for love and help? But realizing that He is our source for mercy will take the pressure off others and free them up to love the best they can.

God, You are the One I will look to for compassion and kindness. You will be my source. In the name of Jesus. Amen.

Depending on God above All Else

When struck by fear, I let go, depending securely upon You alone. In God—whose word I praise—in God I place my trust. I shall not let fear come in, for what can measly men do to me?

PSALM 56:3–4 VOICE

What if we followed the example set by the psalmist regarding fear? Instead of turning into a control freak, the psalmist let go of the wheel. He didn't go into fix-it mode or try to manipulate the situation. He didn't hibernate or stick his head in the sand. He didn't run to others, lamenting about his circumstances to anyone who would listen. He didn't point the finger of blame. He didn't get all tangled up by insecurities and spiral into despair. The psalmist let go, depending on God above all else. What a blessing to know He is trustworthy and faithful!

God, give me courage to let go of the situations that scare me, giving them to You instead. Help me trust You to take the lead so I don't have to fumble my way through the mess. Keep me close by so I feel Your presence. I praise You for being faithful without fail. In the name of Jesus. Amen.

You Are Righteous

But let all the righteous be glad! Yes, let them all rejoice in your presence and be carried away with gladness. Let them laugh and be radiant with joy!

PSALM 68:3 TPT

Praise the Lord you can be righteous when you receive Jesus as your Savior! Even with a track record of bad decisions and terrible choices, you aren't disqualified. God always makes a way for us to be included in the family, and what a beautiful promise it is. For you to be righteous simply means you are right with God. It's not that you're expected to be perfect but rather that you purpose to live according to His will. You follow His commands with intention. You care about what He asks of those who love Him. And you carry your faith into every relationship, every job site, every interaction, and in every quiet moment with the Lord. Your intentionality glorifies Him!

God, what an honor to be righteous in Your eyes. Let my life be an act of praise as I try to point others to You with my words and actions. Let them see my joy and want it for themselves! In the name of Jesus. Amen.

God's Fountain of Forgiveness

God, give me mercy from your fountain of forgiveness! I know your abundant love is enough to wash away my guilt. Because your compassion is so great, take away this shameful guilt of sin. Forgive the full extent of my rebellious ways, and erase this deep stain on my conscience.

PSALM 51:1–2 TPT

Praise God for showing us the mercy we need to wash away the guilt and shame that often plague us. We know full well when we've done something that doesn't benefit us or glorify the Lord. The Holy Spirit within us gives a gut check when our choices don't align with His will. And while guilt says we've done something wrong and shame says we are wrong, God is described as a fountain of forgiveness who will wash it all away when we ask. What an awesome God to make a way for us to live free from that kind of bondage. Even more, He has no expectation of perfection, so extending grace through Jesus comes naturally to Him.

God, thank You for Your abundant love that washes me clean and removes the guilt and shame that come from living outside of Your will. In the name of Jesus. Amen.

Who Do You Need God to Be?

To the fatherless he is a father. To the widow he is a champion friend. The lonely he makes part of a family. The prisoners he leads into prosperity until they sing for joy. This is our Holy God in his Holy Place! But for the rebels there is heartache and despair.

PSALM 68:5–6 TPT

Who do you need the Lord to be to you right now? Do you need Him to be a father to your children who are orphaned? Do you need Him to fill the gaps left by your husband? Do you need His wisdom or discernment? Do you need God to illuminate the right path for you to follow? Do you need Him to be your confidant? Scripture tells us He is willing and able to meet every need we may face. So be bold in your requests, and lift your voice to the heavens for help. And worship Him in those moments as you wait expectantly for God to show up!

God, I am in awe of the lengths You'll go to for those who love You. Thank You for meeting my needs, even the ones that feel silly at times. In the name of Jesus. Amen.

Regardless of Your Emotions

Why am I so overwrought, why am I so disturbed? Why can't I just hope in God? Despite all my emotions, I will believe and praise the One who saves me, my God.

PSALM 42:11 VOICE

We all go through tough seasons when we struggle to place our hope in the Lord. We may be weighed down by relationship problems or feel helpless as we try to navigate a challenging parenting phase. We may be overwhelmed by financial strains to the point that we can see no way out. We may be disturbed by difficult news we can't make sense of in our minds, and the hopelessness lingers. And rather than press into God, looking to Him for a way out of the pit we're stuck in, we wave the white flag of defeat. But like the psalmist, raise a hallelujah anyway. Regardless of your emotions, let your faith rise up to overtake the negatives. Trust God right in the middle of your mess. And praise Him for who He is and His promise to save.

God, I want to give up, but I'm choosing to reach for You instead. Help me find my footing once again. In the name of Jesus. Amen.

He Gives and Takes Away

I was naked, with nothing, when I came from my mother's womb; and naked, with nothing, I will return to the earth. The Eternal has given, and He has taken away. May the name of the Eternal One be blessed.

JOB 1:21 VOICE

When we realize the rush to collect toys and trophies here on earth is futile, we're freed up to focus on storing up treasures in heaven. The truth is, we can't take anything with us, so why are we trying so hard? When we understand that God is the One who gives and takes away according to His will, we won't feel the need to grip the steering wheel so tightly. We can find peace in knowing God is the One who is in control. Even more, everything He does is to benefit us and glorify His name. Let's praise Him for being all-powerful. Let's raise a hallelujah for His omnipotence!

God, give me reminders that my focus while on earth is to be eternal. There's no need to hold the things of this world so tightly. Let me glorify Your name by keeping my heart on eternity. In the name of Jesus. Amen.

Consumed with Awe

God, we are consumed with awe, trembling before you as your glory streams from your Holy Place. The God of power shares his mighty strength with Israel and with all his people. God, we give our highest praise to you!

PSALM 68:35 TPT

When was the last time you were consumed with awe? When was the last time you were wonderstruck by something extraordinary? Was it when you found out you were pregnant? Maybe it was when someone gifted you something completely unexpected. Maybe it was when your special-needs child crossed the finish line. Maybe it was being with a parent as they passed peacefully from this world. Witnessing God's glory shining in our life will be even more breathtaking. It will bring deep reverence as we are filled with unmatched amazement. And it will be the perfect opportunity to raise a hallelujah in worship of God's splendor. Never lose the childlike faith that delights in all He is.

God, anything this world offers, Your gifts are better. No matter how wonderful the moment, time with You trumps it. Let me always be consumed with awe. In the name of Jesus. Amen.

It's Time to Step Out of the Traffic

"Step out of the traffic! Take a long, loving look at me, your High God, above politics, above everything." Jacob-wrestling God fights for us, God-of-Angel-Armies protects us.

PSALM 46:10–11 MSG

Today's verse is a gift because it reminds us to step aside and let God be God. Too often we get right in the middle of our mess and try to work it out ourselves. We gird ourselves for battle, acting as commander in chief in charge of executing the battle plan. But the Lord is the One who is in control. He is the One who promises to protect. God is the One who will save us from destruction. We can raise a hallelujah with confidence because we know, by faith, that God will bring us safely through the battle to the other side. Friend, step out of the traffic and allow the Lord to do what only He can do to remedy the situation you're in. You are held.

God, give me the confidence to step aside and let You be God. Remind me that I am not capable of doing the amazing things You are. I want to embrace every promise You have for me. In the name of Jesus. Amen.

Forgiving Yourself

For I'm so ashamed. I feel such pain and anguish within me.
I can't get away from the sting of my sin against you, Lord!
Everything I did, I did right in front of you, for you saw it all.
Against you, and you above all, have I sinned. Everything you
say to me is infallibly true and your judgment conquers me.

PSALM 51:3–4 TPT

It's normal to feel ashamed when we take a sharp left turn away from God and His commands. There is reason to feel a sense of guilt for choosing defiance, sinning right in the face of the Lord. But we can thank Him for being a God of second chances. We get do-overs when we mess up. God's love for us never wavers and always rejoices over us. And when we take our bad choices and destructive decisions to Him, the Lord will speak truth into our spirit, reminding us of who we are. God will conquer us with His love, drawing us closer as we repent. What an awesome God who is willing to help us get back on track with our faith!

*God, please give me the courage to forgive myself
and try again. In the name of Jesus. Amen.*

God Catches Every Tear

You've kept track of all my wandering and my weeping. You've stored my many tears in your bottle—not one will be lost. For they are all recorded in your book of remembrance.

PSALM 56:8 TPT

Praise the Lord for keeping every tear that falls from our eyes because they are important enough to Him to be bottled. In those moments when you thought no one cared to see your pain, God did. When you cried on the drive home, or quietly into your pillow, or in the shower to drown out the noise, He saw. When you blamed allergies for red eyes and blotchy cheeks, He knew the real reason for the pain spilling out. Friend, God cares so deeply for your heart. Your sadness never goes unnoticed, even when those around you cannot see. Every tear you cry is recorded because it marks an important memory for the Lord. Take a moment to thank Him for being so tenderhearted with you. Let Him know how much it means to you that you're in His thoughts every moment of every day.

God, no one loves me like You do. Thank You for seeing my value! In the name of Jesus. Amen.